LEGAL REASONING

Collected Essays

Contemporary European Cultural Studies
Gianni Vattimo and Santiago Zabala,
Series Editors

This series publishes English translations of works by contemporary European intellectuals from philosophy, religion, politics, law, ethics, aesthetics, social sciences, and history. Volumes included in this series will not be included simply for their specific subject matter, but also for their ability to interpret, describe, explain, analyze, or suggest theories that recognize its historicity. Proposals and suggestions for this series should be directed to:

The Davies Group Publishers
PO Box 440140
Aurora, Colorado, 80044–0140
US

Manfred Frank, *The Boundaries of Agreement*
Antonio Livi, *Reasons for Believing*
Jósef Ni nik, *The Arbitrariness of Philosophy*
Paolo Crocchiolo, *The Amorous Tinder*
José Guimón, *Art and Madness*
Darío Antiseri, *Poppers Vienna*
Remo Bodei, *Logics of Delusion*
Philip Larrey, *Thinking Logically*
Giovanni Mari, *The Postmodern, Democracy, History*
Emanuela Fornari, *Modernity Out of Joint*
Duncan Kennedy, *Legal Reasoning*
Ana Messuti, *Time As Punishment*

LEGAL REASONING

Collected Essays

Duncan Kennedy

A volume in the series
Contemporary European Cultural Studies
Gianni Vattimo and Santiago Zabala, Editors.

The Davies Group, Publishers
Aurora, Colorado

Library of Congress Cataloging-in-Publication Data

Kennedy, Duncan, 1942-
  Legal reasoning : collected essays / Duncan Kennedy.
    p. cm. -- (Contemporary European cultural studies)
  Includes index.
  ISBN 978-1-934542-02-6 (alk. paper)
  1. Law--Methodology. 2. Law--United States--Methodology. I. Title.
  K213.K46 2007
  340'.11--dc22
                    2008000716

Printed in the United States of America
Published 2008. The Davies Group Publishers, Aurora, CO

0123456789

Contents

Introduction   1

Freedom and Constraint in Adjudication:
    A Critical Phenomenology   11

A Semiotics of Legal Argument   87

A Left/Phenomenological Alternative to the
    Hart/Kelsen Theory of Legal Interpretation   153

Thoughts on Coherence, Social Values and
    National Tradition in Private Law   175

Index   213

INTRODUCTION

The four articles collected in this book present an account of legal reasoning, beginning with the practices of jurists in the American common law system. Throughout, I've tried to compare my version of American practice with alternative European and American theoretical positions and with European practice. The account is phenomenological. It describes the experience of legal reasoning while suspending or "bracketing" the question of the "essence," meaning, in the case of legal reasoning, the question what is "truly" the law that applies to any particular case.

As far as I know, "Freedom and Constraint in Adjudication: A Critical Phenomenology," the first of the pieces collected here, is the only extant attempt to apply this methodology, derived from Husserl via Sartre's *Being and Nothingness*, to the practices of jurists. This origin may make the account seem exotic in the context of the academic discipline of legal theory. It draws extensively, nonetheless, on the legal realist writings that were obsessed with the question of "what judges do." Karl Llewellyn, Felix Cohen and Edward Levi are important sources. The mode of presentation is novelistic rather than philosophical or technically legal.

While "Freedom and Constraint" is an overview, the second essay, "A Semiotics of Legal Argument," focuses in on one aspect of the reasoning process. It proposes that we understand the juristic practice of non-deductive legal argument about the proper interpretation of a rule, or about the choice of a rule where there is an acknowledged gap or conflict, through the analogy of the langue/parole distinction in Saussurian linguistics.

To this end, it presents a partial "lexicon" of the "argument bites," or stock non-deductive arguments, used by jurists in opinions, briefs and scholarly writing. For example, "your proposed rule is too vague to be administrable," or "your proposed rule is too rigid to produce equitable outcomes." Along with the lexicon, the article identifies the "operations" through which jurists generate whole arguments that are readily intelligible ("meaningful") as instances ("parole") of correct legal speech. This piece portrays these operations as having a peculiar dialectical or reversible character, as in the two argument bites above. As a consequence, skill in legal argument will often permit one to neutralize an opponent, or turn the tables, through the mechanical process of producing the paired opposite of his argument.

As with the phenomenological approach of the first essay, the semiotic approach of the second has both an extensive European genealogy and roots in legal realism, particularly in Llewellyn's famous article "Canons on Statutes," which did for the maxims of statutory interpretation what the first part of "A Semiotics of Legal Argument" tries to do for policy argument broadly understood. Unlike "Freedom and Constraint," this second piece deals, in an appendix, with its Continental philosophical and American legal theoretical origins. A second appendix addresses four "European objections" to the approach of the article that I encountered quite frequently when I first began to present it at scholarly meetings over there.

The semiotic study is in a sense phenomenological. It is, after all, about the experience of legal reasoning. The claim that the practice of non-deductive legal argument proceeds in a manner that is well analogized to speech in a primary language, with a lexicon, rules of transformation, grammatical and syntactical rules, and so forth, is a claim about what legal argument feels like from the inside. It is an assertion about how jurists experience it, rather than a claim about what it is in essence.

But there is also an interesting analogy between the phenomenological methodology of the first piece and the semiotic methodology of the second. The second approach makes a bracketing move, just as the first does. The phenomenologist brackets the question of the essence of the legal norm: the question "what is the valid legal rule governing this case" is set aside as unanswerable. For the semiotician, the study of legal argument requires us to bracket the question of the correctness, or plausibility, or weight of non-deductive arguments while trying to figure out what they all share as instances of parole in the same langue.

All that counts is determining the lexicon and the operations the practitioners must deploy if the argument is to be a "correct legal" one. But "correct," here, does not mean "legally correct," only "correctly legal," just as we can identify a sentence as in correct English without having an opinion as to its truth or falsity.

The effect of the two bracketing moves is supposed to be to change our understanding of what it is like to be compelled by legal reasoning, or for legal reasoning to "determine" the correct answer to the question what legal norm applies to a case. The phenomenological account is supposed to persuade the reader that jurists often destabilize their initial experience of legal compulsion by legal work. They work with that very intention, for one agenda or another, in the hopes of making the legally determined legally undetermined, or for that matter, in the other direction, to make an initial experience of undetermination turn into its opposite.

The semiotic account, in so much as it convinces that the effect of legal necessity produced by a legal argument is often reversible by a jurist skilled in the operations, is a case study of one of the specific kinds of legal work that can produce these results. It is an account of just how a jurist can go about making the determinate indeterminate and vice versa.

The two pieces together represent the experience of legal reasoning as an activity pursued in a medium that is at once plastic and resistant. They do *not* aim to show that legal reasoning is always indeterminate, or that there is always a good argument for whatever legal result the jurist wants to achieve. They are firmly positioned against "global indeterminacy" theses. They likewise reject the notion that we can meaningfully state that law is "most of the time" or "generally" determinate. Given the phenomenological bracketing already referred to and the ever present possibility of argumentative work, such statements are meaningless.

On this basis, the account has to do with politics in two senses. The first is that it presents political ideology as an important
element in the interpretive activity of many jurists, particularly in
cases where there are high political stakes of one kind or another.
The second is that the account is itself part of my own particular left/modernist-postmodernist political project (as well as part
of what I don't blush to call a "scientific" inquiry into the subject
matter).

In "Freedom and Constraint," I try to imagine what it would
be like to be a judge. The vehicle for the account is a novelistic
presentation of what I imagine it would be like for me to be a judge
in a United States District Court confronted with a case in which,
according to my first impression, the obviously applicable legal rule
will not permit me to decide the case the way my political convictions tell me it should be decided if there were no binding legal
norm already applicable.

The goal is to describe convincingly the way in which the judge's
personal convictions about justice enter into the decision process.
They do so, in my account, as what orients the direction of the
judge's work of interpretation, rather than as an external factor that
simply determines it. They motivate work in the at once plastic and
resistant medium of law. Moreover, in this account, the personal
political views of the judge are in part caused by his prior exposure
to the legal order he interprets, as well as an important influence
on how he does that interpretation. The result is that the judge's
work may end by reversing rather than allowing the realization of
his personal agenda.

In other words, political ideology is no more an outside, external determinant, than it is an excluded irrelevance. Moreover,
political ideology is no more a self-applying text than is the law.
The judge will have to work to decide what his personal political
convictions require in the case at hand. Like the work of legal
interpretation, this will involve unsettling experiences of determinacy and indeterminacy, rather than the simple application of
principle. Note that I am not claiming that all legal reasoning is

politically oriented, just that that is sometimes the case and some-times with very high stakes.

This way of looking at the role of politics in legal reasoning struck me as worth developing at much greater length, and I did that in *A Critique of Adjudication [fin de siecle]*. I have summarized the argument of that book, and fitted it together with these phe-nomenological and semiotic pieces, in the very short, highly con-densed "A Left Phenomenological Alternative to the Hart/Kelsen Theory of Legal Interpretation."

That essay, as the title indicates, is also an attempt to situate the account in mainstream legal theory by contrasting it sharply with the "core/penumbra" understanding of legal reasoning. The last essay, "Thoughts on Coherence, Social Values and National Tradition in Private Law," does the same for the named conceptions as they figure in the current discourse on the Europeanization of private law. My hope is that the rather elaborate attempts through-out the book to figure out how my account resembles and differs from the more familiar American, Anglo-American and Continen-tal European accounts will make it more intelligible, and easier to critique constructively, than it would be if presented as a tub on its own bottom, so to speak.

The second sense in which these essays have to do with politics concerns their objective rather than their content. They were con-ceived as part of a left/modernist-postmodernist ideological proj-ect. The left element means radical egalitarianism and participa-tory democracy. Modernism-postmodernism refers to cultural and aesthetic modernism and its critique, rather than to the Enlighten-ment. It is a project of avant garde experimentation aimed, always within a limiting context, at emotional/intellectual/aesthetic tran-scendence of convention.

For both the leftist and the modernist/post-modernist parts of the project, a critique of legal certainty of the type developed in this book seems liberatory. First of all, it seems clear to me, as a leftist contemplating the possibilities for radical social transforma-tion, that one obstacle is the reification or fetishization of law. By this I mean not that people wish to be governed by law, but that the intensity of the wish leads them to overestimate what law does or could do to explain or justify social practices. The point of the critique is that both the standard version of the rule of law and the standard version of liberal constitutionalism with judicial review, as purported descriptions of liberal reality and as ideals, lose plausibility, to put it modestly, when we take account of the under-determinate character of legal reasoning.

One might find this argument convincing even if one were a committed liberal, or a conservative or a libertarian. In other words, there is nothing inherently leftist about it. It is part of a left project not because it is inherently leftist but because in the current state of politics in the world, it seems to me that fetishized or reified belief in the rule of law is an obstacle to leftist conviction and activism. In this respect, I have the opposite assessment from those who see undermining legal fetishism as undermining leftist faith.

At a more abstract level, all of the essays operate in the anti-liberal tradition of Feuerbach and Marx, and also of rightist critics of the Rights of Man as the goal or *terminus ad quem* of the project of emancipation. In this tradition, liberal false necessity, including in particular legal necessity, is always an obstacle to emancipation, because belief is flight into fantasy, at the same time that it is an impediment to analysis.

The phenomenological/semiotic/ideological critique of legal reasoning fits into the modernist-postmodernist project in a somewhat different way. To the extent the account is convincing, it pushes toward a particular kind of thinking about the ethics of situations in which one has a duty to obey the law. One might call it an anarchist mode, because if the analysis is right, it puts actors who we normally think of as obligated to obey the law in the position of not being able to do that, or at least not being able to do it in a way that decisively or clearly subordinates them to a law maker other than themselves.

What law there is to obey, even granting a full commitment to obedience, will vary according to how much work, with what work strategy, and what skill, they bring to bear on the initial perception that a particular legal norm clearly binds under the circumstances. This means that the jurist has to decide *in every case* how to orient his or her work or non-work. The jurist has to do this without being able to rely on the notion of fidelity to law to answer the question. This decision on a work orientation may (or, of course, may not) have important social, economic, political or cultural consequences.

That it may turn out to be an unimportant decision does not mean that the jurist can avoid it, or avoid responsibility if the consequences turn out to be significant. It is as though every case were at least initially within the category denominated in the first article of the Swiss Civil Code as requiring the judge to decide as he would if he were a legislator. Or as though the law has always already "run out" at the moment the jurist sets out to interpret.

So in what sense anarchist? First, because an enlightened jurist can't believe of himself that he does what he does because subject to the role constraint of obedience to law, that is to the state. It is true that there is such a role constraint and that it may or may not in the end determine his action. But it is also possible that the role constraint that he must seek justice will turn him into a law maker no matter how much he doesn't want that responsibility. It may require him to do at least a little potentially destabilizing legal work whenever his initial sense is that the obvious interpretation of the law makes it an instrument of injustice.

Anarchist also in the stronger sense that where the actor is playing a decision making role in a private institution, corporate in one sense or another (for profit or not, etc.), the same set of questions and dilemmas arise. The institution will have a mission and a mission statement, some claim to be ethically situated even if only as a profit maker for shareholders. Actors are agents, just as in the state context. The actor/agent will have to decide, according to his or her personal convictions, in which direction to work when interpreting the mission statement.

The notion is that all these decision makers who supposedly, in principle, are bound by the law or by the charter of the particular private entity they are part of, are constantly exercising a denied discretion in choosing a work strategy. Once I've acknowledged this, my thought is that I have to start taking responsibility for the discretion. I can't lodge it outside myself. My political program as a legal reasoner becomes to do the reasoning in such a way that I advance the good.

My idea is that this decision has to be political in the strongest Weberian sense: the ethic is what Weber calls "the ethic of responsibility" meaning responsibility for all the consequences, without being able to appeal to a coherent and socially accepted set of criteria of justification for the decision. The role constraint is no more than "do your best under all the circumstances to do something politically good."

If I am to decide in full responsibility for all the consequences, I have to take into account the possibility of tacit or overt alliances with other legal reasoners, alliances that may require me to sacrifice what I'd like to see happen in a particular case of legal reasoning in the hope that the long run consequences will be more beneficial than those of sticking to my guns. Again, it seems plain to me that judges and other jurists already do this all the time. But they do it while systematically denying it.

I have, moreover, to take into account what others will likely do with *their* discretion. What I say about, first, my discretion, and, second, about how I propose to exercise it, should be influenced by the consequences for the legal order (and beyond) that I anticipate from their reaction to the way I describe what I am doing. So I may have to confront the classic problem of good faith in my description of what I'm doing—do I misrepresent myself as law following when I experience myself as law constituting? One way in which I think of this book is as an attempt to force this question.

Cambridge, Massachusetts
November 5, 2007

"Freedom and Constraint in Adjudication: A Critical Phenomenology" was first published in Volume 36 of the *Journal of Legal Education*, in 1986. A shorter version appeared in Allan Hutchinson & Patrick Monahan, eds., *The Rule of Law: Ideal or Ideology?* (Toronto: Carswell, 1987). Both of these versions have serious typos, which I corrected when the full piece was reprinted in James Boyle, ed., *Critical Legal Studies* (Aldershot, U.K.: Dartmouth, 1992). That version is reproduced here. There is a Spanish translation in book form: *Libertad y restriccion en la decision judicial: El debate con la teoria critica del derecho (CLS)*, Diego Eduardo López, trans., con un "Estudio preliminar" de César Rodríguez (Bogota, Colombia: Siglo del Hombre Editores, 1999).

"A Semiotics of Legal Argument" first appeared in an incomplete tentative version in Roberta Kevelson, ed., *Law and Semiotics*, Volume 3 (New York: Plenum Press, 1989). I finished it and added the first appendix for publication in Volume 42 of the *Syracuse Law Review*, in 1991. I added a "European Introduction," appearing here as a second appendix, for the reprinting of the article in 3 *Collected Courses of the Academy of European Law*, Book 2, 309-365 (Amsterdam: Kluwer Academic Publishers, 1994).

An earlier version of "A Left Phenomenological Alternative to the Hart/Kelsen Theory of Legal Interpretation" was published, under the title "A Left Phenomenological Critique of the Hart/Kelsen Theory of Legal Interpretation" in Caceres et al, eds., *Problemas contemporaneas de la filosofia del derecho* (Mexico City: UNAM, 2005). A Dutch translation appeared as "Een linkse fenomenologische kritiek op de rechtsvindingstheorie van Hart en Kelsen," 3 *Nederlands tijdschrift voor Rechtsfilosofie & Rechtstheorie* 242 (2004). An earlier draft of the version included in this volume appeared in 40 *Kritische Justiz* 296 (2007)

"Thoughts on Coherence, Social Values and National Tradition in Private Law" was first published as a chapter in Martijn Hesselink, ed., *The Politics of a European Civil Code* (Amsterdam: Kluwer Law International, 2006).

FREEDOM AND CONSTRAINT IN ADJUDICATION

A CRITICAL PHENOMENOLOGY

This paper attempts to describe the process of legal reasoning as I imagine I might do it if I were a judge assigned a case that initially seemed to present a conflict between "the law" and "how-I-want-to-come-out." Such a description, if at all true to experience, may be helpful in assessing the various claims about and images of law that figure in jurisprudential, political, and social theoretical discussion. It may also be helpful in assessing what law teachers teach future lawyers about the nature of the materials they will use in their profession. But I will have little to say about these implications, aside from a polemical Afterword.[1]

I am not sure what difference it makes to the phenomenology of adjudication whether I begin with this situation rather than another. The whole experience of law may be sufficiently the same thing through and through so that wherever you start, you end up with approximately the same picture. Or it may be that there is no experience of legality that's constant without regard to role and initial posture of the case. What I am convinced of is the need to start with some particularization. I don't find myself at all convinced when people start out claiming they can tell us about judging without some grounding in a specific imagined situation.

The judge is a federal district court judge in Boston. I am from Boston. I'm more a ruling class elite type than a local politician or notable type, which is why I choose the federal forum. But what's most important is that the judge is responsible for deciding this case, rather than a party or an observer or an advocate. I am going to be looking at law as a person who will have to apply it, interpret it, change it, defy it, or whatever. I will do this in the context of the legal and lay community that follows what federal district court judges do, and with the possibility of appeal always present to my mind.

The more complex conditions of this inquiry have to do with the polarity between my initial impression of "the law" and my initial sense of how-I-want-to-come-out. How-I-want-to-come-out might be based on my having been bribed and wanting to keep my bargain, or on a sense of what decision would be popular with my community (legal or local), or on what I thought the appeals court would likely do in the case of an appeal. It might be based on a sense that the equities of this particular case are peculiar because they favor an outcome different from what the law requires, even though the law is basically a very good one, and even though it was on balance a good decision to frame it so inflexibly that it couldn't adjust to take account of these particular equities.

Or it might be that I disagree with the way the law here resolves the problem of exceptional situations, believing that it could have been crafted to be flexible to take care of this case. Or it could be that I see the law here as "unfair" in the sense that, taking the rest of the system at face value, it would be better to change this rule. This rule might be an anomaly. (Later I will take up the question of the rules about the judge changing the rules.)

Instead of any of these objections, imagine that I think the rule that seems to apply is bad because it strikes the wrong balance between two identifiable conflicting groups, and does so as part of a generally unjust overall arrangement that includes many similar rules, all of which ought in the name of justice to change. I mean to suggest a "political" objection to the law, and a how-I-want-to-come-out that is part of a general plan of opposition.

Again, the experience of legality may well be different according to the character of the "I want" that opposes "the law." All I insist on is this: it is useless to discuss the conflict of "personal preference vs. law" without specifying what kind of preference we are dealing with.

✧   ✧   ✧

Here's what I mean by my initial impression that the law requires a particular outcome. Suppose there is a strike of union bus drivers going on in Boston. The company hires nonunion drivers and sets out to resume service. On the first day, union members lie down in the street outside the bus station to prevent the buses from passing. They do not disturb the general flow of traffic, and they are nonviolent. The local police arrest them and cart them off, but this takes hours. They are charged with disturbing the peace and obstructing a public way (misdemeanors) and released on light bail. The next day other union members obstruct, with similar results. The buses run, but only late and amid a chaotic jumble. The company goes into federal court for an injunction against the union tactic.

When I first think about this case, not being a labor law expert, but having some general knowledge, I think, "There is no way they will be able to get away with this. The rule of law is going to be that workers cannot prevent the employer from making use of the buses during the strike. The company will get its injunction."

I disagree with this imagined rule. I don't think management should be allowed to operate the means of production [m.o.p.] with substitute labor during a strike. I think there should be a rule that until the dispute has been resolved, neither side can operate the m.o.p. without the permission of the other (barring various kinds of extraordinary circumstances). This view is part of a general preference for transforming the current modes of American economic life in a direction of greater worker self-activity, worker control and management of enterprise, in a decentralized setting that blurs the lines between "owner" and "worker," and "public" and "private" enterprise.

My feeling that the law is against me in this case is a quick intuition about the way things have to be. I haven't actually read any cases or articles that describe what the employer can and can't do with the m.o.p. during a strike. I vaguely remember *In Dubious Battle,* a Steinbeck classic I read when I was 16. But I would bet money that some such rule exists.

If there is a rule that the employer can do what he wants with the m.o.p., I think it will probably turn out that there is relief in federal court (under the rubric of unfair labor practices?). If relief is available, I have a strong feeling that the workers threaten irreparable injury to the employer, so that he can show the various things usually required to justify an injunction. But I also vaguely remember that federal courts aren't supposed to issue injunctions in labor disputes.

There is lots of uncertainty here. I am not sure that a federal district court has jurisdiction under the labor law statutes to intervene on the employer's behalf when the local authorities are already enforcing the local general law about obstructing public ways. I am not sure that if there is a basis for federal intervention an injunction is appropriate. I will have to look into all these things before I'm at all sure how this case will or should come out.

On the other hand, I am quite sure the employer can use the m.o.p. as he pleases. And I am quite, quite sure that if there is such a rule, then the workers have violated it here. I am sure that what I mean by the rule is that the employer has both a privilege to act and a right to protection against interference, and that what the workers' did here was interference.

Since the supposed rule of law that I don't like won't get applied so as to lead to an injunction unless all the uncertainties are resolved against the workers, I do not yet confront a direct conflict between the law and how-I-want-to-come-out. But I already have the feeling of "the law" as a constraint on me. It's time to ask what that means.

✧ ✧ ✧

The initial apparent objectivity of the objectionable rule

I use the word objectivity here to indicate that from my point of view the *application of the rule to this case* feels like a nondiscretionary, necessary, compulsory procedure. I can no more deny that, if there is such a rule, the workers have violated it, than I can deny that I am at this minute in Cambridge, Massachusetts, sitting on a chair, using a machine called a typewriter. The rule just applies itself. What I *meant* by interfering with the owner's use of the m.o.p. was workers lying down in the street when the employer tries to drive the buses out to resume service during the strike. I'm sure from the description that the workers actually intended to do exactly what the rule says they have no right to do.

Note that this sense of objectivity is internal—it's what happens in my head. But the minute I begin to think about the potential conflict between the law and how-I-want-to-come-out a quite different question will arise. How will other people see this case, supposing that the preliminary hurdles are overcome?

Sometimes it will seem to me that everyone (within the relevant universe) will react to this case as one to which the rule applies. I imagine them going through the same process I did, and it is instantly obvious that they too will see the workers as having violated the rule. If this happens, the rule application acquires a double objectivity. The reaction of other people is an anticipated fact like my anticipation that the sun will rise tomorrow or that this glass will break if I drop it on the floor.

It is important not to mush these forms of objectivity together. It is possible for me to see the case as "not clearly governed by the rule" when I do my interior rule application, but to anticipate that the relevant others will see it as "open and shut." And it is possible for me to see it as clear but to anticipate that others will see it as complex and confusing.

The next thing that happens is that I set to work on the problem of this case. I already have, as part of my life as I've lived it up to this moment, a set of intentions, a life-project as a judge, that will orient me among the many possible attitudes I could take to this work.

It so happens that I see myself as a political activist, someone with the "vocation of social transformation," as Roberto Unger put it. I see the set of rules in force as chosen by the people who had the power to make the choices in accord with their views on morality and justice and their own self-interest. And I see the rules as remaining in force because victimized groups have not had the political vision and energy and raw power to change them. I see myself as a focus of political energy for change in an egalitarian, communitarian, decentralized, democratic socialist direction (which doesn't mean these slogans are any help in figuring out what the hell to do in any particular situation).

Given my general orientation, the work I am going to do in this case will have two objectives, which may or may not conflict. I want these specific workers to get away with obstructing the buses, and I want to move the law as much as possible in the direction of allowing workers a measure of legally legitimated control over the disposition of the m.o.p. during a strike.

If my only objective were to avoid an injunction against lying down in front of the buses during this strike, I would be tempted toward a strategy that would allow me to avoid altogether the apparent legal rule forbidding worker interference. I could just delay, in the hope that the workers will win the strike before I'm forced to rule. I could focus on developing a new version of the facts, and hope to deny the injunction on that basis, or I could look for a "technicality" having no apparent substantive relevance (e.g., the statute of frauds, a mistake in the caption of a pleading).

On a more substantive level, I could put my energy into researching the issues of federal jurisdiction and the appropriateness of an injunction. Here, if the effort paid off, I might be able to move the law in a way favorable to workers in general, even though the move wouldn't formally address worker control over the m.o.p. during a strike.

But the strategy I want to discuss here is that of frontal assault on the application of the rule that the workers can't obstruct the company's use of the m.o.p. If this strategy succeeds, the result will be both to get the workers off in this case *and* to accomplish my law reform objective. There will be a small reduction in employers' power to invoke the state apparatus, a change that will be practically useful in future legal disputes over strikes. And the mantle of legal legitimacy will shift a little, from all out endorsement of management prerogatives to a posture that legitimates, to some degree, workers' claims to rights over the m.o.p.

What I see as interesting about the situation as I have portrayed it up to this point is that we are not dealing with a "case governed by a rule," but rather with a perception that a rule probably governs, and that applying the rule will very likely produce a particular (pro-employer) result. The judge is neither free nor bound. I don't see it that way from inside the situation. From inside the situation, the question is, Where am I going to deploy the resources I have available for this case? The issue is how should I direct my *work* to bring about an outcome that accords with my sense of justice. My situation as a judge (initial perceived conflict between "the law" and how-I-want-to-come-out) is thus quite like that of a lawyer who is brought a case by a client and on first run-through is afraid the client will lose. The question is, Will this first impression hold up as I set to work to develop the best possible case on the other side?

Having to work to achieve an outcome is in my view fundamental to the situation of the judge. It is neither a matter of being bound nor a matter of being free. Or, you could say that the judge is both free *and* bound—free to deploy work in any direction but limited by the pseudo-objectivity of the rule-as-applied, which he may or may not be able to overcome.

Isn't what I am doing illegitimate, from the standpoint of legality, right from the start? One could argue that since I think the law favors the company I have no business trying to develop the best possible case for the union. But this misunderstands the rules of the game of legality. All members of the community know that one's initial impression that a particular rule governs and that when applied to the facts it yields X result is *often* wrong. That's what makes law such a trip. What at first looked open and shut is ajar, and what looked vague and altogether indeterminate abruptly reveals itself to be quite firmly settled under the circumstances.

So it is an important part of the role of judges and lawyers to test whatever conclusions they have reached about "the correct legal outcome" by trying to develop the best possible argument on the other side. In my role as an activist judge I am simply doing what I'm supposed to when I test my first impression against the best pro-union argument I can develop.

If I manage to develop a legal argument against the injunction, the ideal of impartiality requires me to test that argument in turn against a newly worked-out best counterargument in favor of the company. Eventually, my time will run out, and I'll just have to decide.

What would betray legality would be to adopt the wrong attitude at the *end* of the reasoning process, when I've reached a conclusion about "what the law requires" and found it still conflicts with how-I-want-to-come-out.

For the moment, I'm free to play around.

The euphoric moment in which I conceive legal reasoning as "playing around with the rule" doesn't last long. What follows is panic as I rack my brain for *any* way around the overwhelming sense that if the rule is "workers can't interfere with the owner's use of the m.o.p. during a strike," then I cannot do anything for the union. I am ashamed of this panic. It's not just that I'm not coming up with anything; I also feel that I *should* be coming up with something. It's a disgrace—it shows I lack legal reasoning ability.

I feel like a fool for trumpeting the indeterminacy of doctrine and claiming to be a manipulative whiz.

As my panic deepens, I begin to consider alternatives. If I can't mount an attack on the rule-as-applied, maybe I will have to research the earlier contract between the union and the bus company. I have a strong feeling that contracts are manipulable if one applies concepts like good faith, implication of terms, and the public interest, all relevant here. Maybe I'll have to try to "read something in." But this approach is clearly less good than going right for the rule itself.

Then I start thinking about the federal injunction aspect of the case, as opposed to the labor tort aspect. I'm sure that the combination of the 1930s anti-injunction statute with federal court injunctive enforcement of at least some terms in collective bargaining agreements (after *Lincoln Mills?* I can't quite remember) must have made a total hash of the question of when federal courts will grant injunctions. If only I could worry just about *that,* I bet I could easily come up with a good pro-worker argument. But that move is also less good than going for the rule.

Then there are the really third-rate solutions based on the hope that the facts will turn out to be at least arguably different than they seemed to be when I first heard about the case, and that the company's lawyers will make a stupid technical mistake.

All the while I'm desperately racking my brains. I think I have good maxims for legal reasoning, but what are they? The rule represents a compromise between two conflicting policies, so there must be a gray area where the terms of the compromise are not clear. But this case seems clear. There are *always* exceptions to the rule. But I can't think of any here.

When an idea starts to come, it just comes, little by little getting clearer, as I work to tease it out, flesh it out, add analogies. Here it is:

Of course (oh, how I love to feel that reassuring "of course" tripping off my tongue at the beginning of an argument), it is not *liter-*

ally true that the workers are forbidden from "interfering with the owners' use of the m.o.p. during a strike." They can picket and use all kinds of publicity measures to dissuade people from riding the company's buses.

Here I begin to lose my grip again. Lying down in the roadway is a far cry from picketing, which doesn't interfere at all *physically* with the company's use of the buses and is after all justified as an exercise of First Amendment rights. This exception won't do me any good.

After more false leads and panic (I try manipulating the concept of "owner" to get the workers a piece of the action, but that tactic just seems to push me into the inferior implied contract route) I come back to my exception. The workers did lie down in the street to block the buses, but they did not intend to and did not in fact use force to prevent them from rolling. After all, they submitted peacefully to arrest. And the press was everywhere. Obviously the worker on the ground *could not have* physically prevented the bus from rolling, because it could have rolled right over him.

Still, on those two days of lie-ins the company failed to resume service in the fashion it had planned. The workers did physically obstruct the owner's use of the m.o.p. and were delighted to do so. The disruption wasn't just a side effect.

On the other hand, maybe I can argue that the demonstration was a symbolic protest, an attempt to (a) exert moral suasion on the company by impressing it with the extreme feeling of the workers and their willingness to take risks, their sense that the company is theirs as much as management's, and (b) a gesture toward the public through the media.

I will emphasize the non-violent civil disobedience aspects: a physical tactic that *could not in fact* have prevented the use of the m.o.p. by the company, and submission to arrest.

I could hold that because of these factors there should be no federal labor law injunctive remedy beyond what is accorded under state law (narrow version). Or that this demonstration is the *exercise* of First Amendment rights, so that injunction of a nonviolent civil disobedient protest would be an unconstitutional restriction of expression, even though it is of course perfectly permissible for the state to arrest the demonstrators and subject them to its normal criminal process (broad version).

By this time, I'm getting high. I have no idea whether this line of argument will work. I have even lost track of exactly how this argument can be brought to bear in the employer's federal court action for an injunction. (This is probably because I've gotten into an argument on the merits before clarifying in my own mind what the basis of federal jurisdiction may be, and before getting into the anti-injunction Wagner Act issue.) But I am nonetheless delighted. My heart lifts because it seems that the work of legal reasoning within my pro-worker project is paying off.

✧   ✧   ✧

What I've tried to do here is to turn this into a First Amendment prior restraint (or at least a "free speech policy") case. I relied on the idea that there had to be some limit to the employer's freedom from interference, came up with picketing by trying to imagine what the workers certainly *could* do to him, and then looked for an extension of the picketing idea to embrace the particular facts of this case.

Another way to put it is that I stopped imagining the rule of "no interference" as the only thing out there—as dominating an empty field and therefore grabbing up and incorporating any new fact situation that had anything at all "sort of like interference" in it. I tried to find the other rules that set the limits of this one, so I could tuck my case under their wing. Once I identified those other affirmative rules (protecting picketing and other First-Amendment-based attacks on the employer's use of the m.o.p.), I re-stated the facts of the lie-in to emphasize those aspects that fit (nonviolence, submission to arrest, one prone body can't stop a Scenicruiser bus unless the Scenicruiser wants to be stopped).

✧   ✧   ✧

The minute I get rolling, new wrinkles occur to me. Maybe we should see the lie-in as an appeal by union workers to the nonunion replacement bus drivers. It is they, not the union members, who actually stop the buses on the street and fail thereby to carry out the company's plan to resume service. It would be all right to try to persuade the nonunion replacements with flyers, to picket them, to threaten them with anger and non-association, to guilt trip them and swear at them. The lie-in is just a small extension of those tactics. It is a physical statement to them. Will this fly? I have no idea. It is part of the brainstorming process, rather than a deduction of the rule that covers the case. It is part of the work of producing lots of alternative ways at the problem, hoping that one of them will break through. I am already wondering whether it's even worth the time to pursue this approach further.

✧   ✧   ✧

As I euphorically contemplate my "breakthrough" from panicked blankness into a swirling plethora of possible legal arguments, I come up against a disturbing thought. By redefining this as a First Amendment case, I have not *abolished* the old rule that once seemed to settle everything. I've just limited its scope. It is still true that (except in these cases I've been discussing) the workers can't interfere with the owner's use of the m.o.p. during a strike. For example, I think, looking now for a core case that will resist my First Amendment foray into the soft periphery of the rule, if the workers went into the company's garage and physically appropriated the buses, that would be clear interference of the type the rule was meant to prevent.

Three reactions to this thought: (a) I'm disappointed that, fantasy aside, my holding could do no more than chip away a little, though a little is not nothing, at the owner's power. (b) Then I worry that the hypothetical I've just constructed is the hypothetical I was afraid the lie-in might be—the hypothetical in which there is just nothing you can do, because if the rule is in force, it applies to the case in an objective, ineluctable way. (c) But then I think, maybe I could unsettle this one too. Let's hypothesize some more facts. And I have a crazy flash to the tort law doctrine of "recapture of chattels" which says that the owner of a chattel can't use force to recapture it from a person who seized it under a claim of right without using force. Suddenly I'm wondering whether that means the employer would have to sue in conversion and go through the whole trial before there would be an order for return of the chattel, supposing the union got hold of it in just the right way. And so on.

The question is not whether my initial off-the-wall legal intuitions turn out to be right. They *may* eventually generate at least superficially plausible legal arguments. But maybe it will turn out that the law is so well settled in another direction that I will have to abandon them and try something else the minute I get out *Gorman on Labor Law* and *Prosser on Torts*. Legal reasoning is a kind of work with a purpose, and here the purpose is to make the case come out the way my sense of justice tells me it ought to, in spite of what seems at first like the *resistance* or *opposition* of "the law."

Resistance or opposition is the characteristic of the law when I anticipate it as a constraint on how-I-want-to-come-out. But if my initial sense had been that the law was "on my side," it would be a resistance or opposition from the point of view of the company. I would experience it as a protective barrier I was building around my position, perhaps, or as armor I need to fit to my particular body so that the other side won't be able to strip it away or penetrate it. If I had no sense of "which way the law goes on this," so that each side had an equal opportunity to make a persuasive legal argument, I might experience the law as a body of raw material out of which to "build my case," or perhaps as a mass of wet clay that two opposing potters are each trying to shape before it hardens.

The image changes according to how the law initially presents itself in relation to how-I-want-to-come-out. But in each case I am suggesting that one of the ways in which we experience law (not the only way, as we'll see) is as a medium in which one pursues a project, rather than as something that tells us what we have to do. When we approach it this way, law constrains as a physical medium constrains—you can't do absolutely anything you want with a pile of bricks, and what you can do depends on how many you have, as well as on your other circumstances. In this sense, that you are building something out of a given set of bricks constrains you, controls you, deprives you of freedom.

On the other hand, the constraint a medium imposes is relative to your chosen project—to your choice of what you want to make. The medium doesn't tell you what to do with it—that you *must* make the bricks into a doghouse rather than into a garden wall. In the same sense, I am free to work in the legal medium to justify the workers' actions against the company. How my argument will look in the end will depend in a fundamental way on the legal materials—rules, cases, policies, social stereotypes, historical images—but this dependence is a far cry from the inevitable determination of the outcome in advance *by the legal materials themselves*.

✧   ✧   ✧

The metaphor of a physical medium does not help us solve the problem of just how constraining the law is. All it does is suggest that we should understand both freedom and constraint as aspects of the experience of work—chosen project constrained by material properties of the medium—rather than thinking in the back of our mind of a transcendentally free subject who "could do anything," contrasted with a robot programmed by the law.

One might accept the notion that legal argument is manipulation of the legal materials understood as a medium and still believe that the medium constrains very tightly. An absolutely basic question is whether there are some outcomes that you just can't reach so long as you obey the internal rules of the game of legal reasoning. These would be "things you just can't make with bricks," or silk purses you can't make with this particular sow's ear.

For the moment, make any assumption you want as to how tightly the medium constrains the message. Perhaps there is only one correct legal result in most cases, or perhaps there are some results that you simply can't reach through correct legal reasoning, or perhaps there will be a legally plausible course of reasoning to justify any result that you might want to reach.

What I want to ask is how, rather than how tightly law constrains, when we understand it as a medium through which my liberal activist judge-self pursues social justice. When we are clearer about this it will be time to ask, first, whether it is ever (or sometimes, or always) possible in the last analysis to have a conflict between the law and how-I-want-to-come-out, and, if so, what the ethics of the conflict may be.

✧   ✧   ✧

My model of constraint is that people (me as a judge) want to back up their statement of a preference for an outcome (the workers should not be enjoined) with an argument to the effect that to enjoin the workers would "violate the law." We can't understand how this desire to legalize my position constrains me without saying something about why I want to do it.

First, I see myself as having promised some diffuse public that I will "decide according to law," and it is clear to me that a minimum meaning of this pledge is that I won't do things for which I don't have a good legal argument. (This statement says nothing about just how tightly this promise constrains me as to the merits).

Second, various people in my community will sanction me severely if I do not offer a good legal argument for my action. It is not just that I may be reversed and will have broken my promise. It is also that both friends and enemies will see me as having violated a role constraint that they approve of (for the most part), and they will make me feel their disapproval.

Third, I want my position to stick. Although I am free to decide the case any way I want in the sense that no one will physically prevent me from entering a decree for either side, I am bound by the appellate court's reaction. By developing a strong legal argument I make it dramatically less likely that my outcome will be reversed.

Fourth, by engaging in legal argument I can shape the outcomes of future cases and influence popular consciousness about what kinds of action are legitimate—as here, for example, I can marginally influence what people think about worker interference with the m.o.p. during a strike.

Fifth, every case is part of my life-project of being a liberal activist judge. What I do in this case will affect my ability to do things in other cases, enhancing or diminishing my legal and political credibility as well as my technical reputation with the various constituencies that will notice.

Sixth, since I see legal argument as a branch of ethical argument, I would like to know for my own purposes how my position looks translated into this particular ethical medium.

I might be able to achieve some of these objectives at least some of the time without engaging in direct challenges to my initial intuition that the law is adverse. I don't want to be absolute about it, since I can conceive situations in which I think I would go quite unhesitatingly for a "non-legal" approach. But there will be many, many situations in which it appears that, if I wish to achieve my goals, the only way or the obviously best way is to try legal argument.

✧ ✧ ✧

Note that I would have to do *something* even if I wanted to grant the injunction. When I say that my first impression of the law is that it favors the employer's case, I mean that I don't anticipate any difficulty in working up a good argument for the injunction. I see that project as easy, as not much work.

By contrast, deciding *not* to enjoin involves not just the work of pushing pencil across paper to get down thoughts already well worked out before I even begin, but the work of creating something out of nothing. This is a cost of deciding for the workers, and it has at least two aspects. First, the work of creating a good legal argument is hard, scary, and time-consuming. I have limited resources in my life as a judge, and the workers are asking me to allocate them here, when I could put them into some other hard case or just spend all my time on easy cases. My limited store of time and energy for the hard work of creating legal arguments that go against my first impression of what the law is constrains me from doing all kinds of things I could do as a judge if I weren't constrained.

I don't want this point to sound minor, because it isn't. There are lots and lots and lots of rules I would like to change or at least reform. If I could do it by fiat, perhaps I would do a lot of it, do it quite fast, and in a way that might be called holistic. But if I have to generate a legal argument for every change, there is no way I can do a lot, do it fast, or do it holistically.

✧   ✧   ✧

The second way in which I experience the law as a constraint in my hypothetical is that it is one of the determinants of what we might call the "legitimacy cost" of deciding for the workers. Just as there are competitors for my time and creativity as a legal arguer, there are also competitors claiming shares of the *mana* or *charisma* or whatever that attends my position as a judge. I have leeways or, to put it another way, the mere fact that I decide something makes people think it was legally right to decide it that way. But there are limits to this legitimating power, and every case raises them.

In our case, assume that *everyone* has the same initial impression that the law favors the employer. If I decide for the employer, people who know that this decision goes against my personal views may grant my decision some increased legitimacy. They may see me as more able to indicate what the correct legal result is in the next case, because they believe I perceived and followed the law in this one, even when I didn't like it.

This factor aside, no one will be able to say much about "what kind of judge he is" from my decision to go along with the collective initial impression. Going along would be costless in terms of legitimacy. My legitimating power is depleted or augmented only when I try to do something out of the ordinary.

✧   ✧   ✧

I imagine this effect to be a function of two aspects of the situation. The first is the degree of "stretch" from our initial impression of the law to the result I decree. The second is the impact on this distance—we might call it the obviousness gap—of my opinion defending my out-of-the-ordinary result.

The greater the initial perception of stretch, the more of my stock of legitimacy is at stake. Of course, the very notion of legitimating power is that I can reduce the perceived distance between what the law requires and what I decree just by decreeing it. That is the nature of my institutional *mana* or *charisma*. But nothing guarantees that my legitimating power will cause people to see this result as the one that was right all along. That outcome depends on how great the stretch was, and in my own case it is likely that the stretch will be much greater than I can overcome just because the president of the United States has put some black robes on me.

If my automatic legitimating power falls short of fully normalizing the outcome, I will lose legitimating power for the next case—my stock will be depleted—unless I devise an opinion (cast as a legal argument) that makes up the deficit, or even increases the stock. In order to make up the deficit I have to write an opinion that will convince the good faith observer struggling to understand what the law is that in fact my result was not out of the ordinary at all. Rather it was a correct perception, albeit a minority perception, of what the law really required all along.

In other words, I can build up my legitimating power through instances of persuading people through legal argument. If they have had the experience of my "being right" before, experiences of my changing their view of the law, then they will be susceptible in the future to believe what I tell them the law is, quite independently of the argument I can muster.

✧   ✧   ✧

The greater the initial distance between my proposed result and what one would expect, the greater the positive value of persuading the observer through legal argument. You will attribute power to me just in the measure that you find yourself saying, "I never thought he could persuade me of *that!*" Even if I don't persuade you, I gain power if you say, "He didn't convince me, but I never thought he could get me to take the proposition seriously, and here I am arguing hard against it!" On the other hand, if the distance was small to begin with, persuading you that I was right in my initial impression will do no more than very marginally increase my store of legitimating power.

I also increase my power to the extent that my persuasive efforts spill over from this particular case and cause you to reassess other outcomes you had thought pre-eminently legally correct. This is my ability to make my case a "leading case" that will be cited over and over in increasingly distant reaches of law-space as the years go by. My name on that opinion is a help the next time I have an unconventional view on the merits, because it has increased my legitimating power even if in the next case I don't have much in the way of an argument.

✧   ✧   ✧

In this very mechanical model of law as a constraint on the judge, I find myself in a *situation,* defined by my initial impressions of what the law is and of how-I-want-to-come-out. In this situation, I have to decide how I want to allocate my energy among "causes," and estimate the consequences for my project as an activist judge of deciding one way or another.

The constraint imposed by the law is that it defines the distance that I will have to work through in legal argument if I decide to come out the way I initially thought I wanted to. "The law" constrains in that it is an element of the situation as I initially experience it. It is the "field" of my action.

In describing the work of legal reasoning, I have thus far kept to the drastically simplified situation in which there is a rule, a case that the rule appears to cover, and a counter-rule that is initially beyond the periphery of awareness. We need to complicate things.

In my previous examples I treated the rules as autonomous entities that were there in my consciousness independent of cases. I think this treatment corresponds to the way I experience legal rules in real life. It is not true that they are inductive derivations from cases or that they are predictions of what the courts will do. They are much less than either of these: they are verbal formulae I think I know to be "valid" (even though I am often not sure what that means and always aware that my knowledge may turn out to be superficial) that are present like so many random objects floating around in my mind.

One can get access to dozens or hundreds of them—such as "the workers can't interfere with the m.o.p. during a strike"—without having to justify them independently through any inductive or pragmatic process. They are just things we learned in law school or from the newspapers or from reading treatises or from reading cases. They are primary not derivative entities in legal consciousness.

We cite cases as authority for rules. But we also use cases to fill in the actual meaning of the rule when it is open to doubt. In other words, though the rules exist independently of the cases, it is also true that some cases are an essential part of our understanding of what the law of the field "is." This means that decided cases are part of the medium I have to shape if I want to make a persuasive legal argument that the workers shouldn't be enjoined from lying down in front of the buses.

The cases that are most obviously part of the meaning of a rule, rather than mere applications of it, are those we currently see as marking its boundary with a counter-rule. Suppose we have an earlier labor case in which the question was whether there was a First Amendment right to mass picketing, and the courts ruled that there was not, and that the activity should be enjoined as an unfair labor practice or as a tortious interference with the employer's right to use the m.o.p. during a strike. That case is "on the boundary" if it is the "furthest" the employer's right has been extended and the furthest the workers' right of expression has been cut back. If a mass picketing case were followed by a case holding that individual picketing is also tortious, then that case would be the one on the boundary, *if* I perceived individual picketing as at the same time less of an interference with the employer's property rights, and more plausibly a protected speech activity.

The process by which we arrange the cases into a pattern along the boundary, and also within the undisputed territory of one rule or the other, should be understood as a gestalt process. When someone describes the cases, I non-reflectively grasp them as arranging themselves into a particular constellation. For example, I might just instantly understand that mass picketing is more of an interference than individual picketing, and that a lie-in blocking the street is more of an interference than either.

But it does not always happen that the cases arrange themselves for me into neat constellations. For example, I might perceive mass picketing as more of an interference than individual picketing, but also think it more rather than less deserving of

First Amendment protection. After all, mass picketing involves associational as well as speech rights. I might then find it hard to arrange these two types of cases along the boundary between expressive and property rights: maybe they occupy adjoining sectors of the boundary?

The point of this discussion is that our new case, *as it initially presents itself to consciousness,* is situated in a field that contains not only a rule that appears to cover it (no interference with the m.o.p. during a strike) but also many instantiating cases. These appear to establish the rule's meaning. For example, if a case has established that you can't mass picket, then you "obviously" can't obstruct the buses by lying down in the street.

In my initial example of legal reasoning, all I had to do in order to tuck this case under the wing of the counter-principle of free speech was restate both the free speech rule and the facts, until the first covered the second. But if there are decided cases along the boundary I am trying to "move" through restatement, I have to deal with them, unless my restatement of the rule leaves them "undisturbed." I have to "move" them by restating their facts and their holdings until they fit my new formulation of the general rule.

"Movement" is possible because these arrangements that seem so objective as they initially present themselves to consciousness are not in fact anywhere near as solid as chairs or tables. It is a common experience that the constellation shifts or dissolves as one contemplates it. It is also much more common with gestalts of this kind than with the dining room furniture arrangement that you can persuade me, by mustering images and moral arguments, that my initial perception was all wrong. Contrary to my first impression, you argue, mass picketing is "really" more protectable than individual picketing. I hope to persuade you that, contrary to both our initial impressions, the lie-in to block the buses was more worthy of protection than either mass or individual picketing.

✧   ✧   ✧

It may be useful, or at least amusing, to extend the metaphor of the field in order to distinguish between manipulating the facts of a precedent and manipulating the holding. I imagine the facts of the case (I learned them from the opinion or from somewhere else, such as a classroom or a newspaper) as defining *the position of the case in the field of law.* We may grasp that position as close to a boundary line, or on it, or as so far within the boundary that these facts seem "easy" and the general rule just "applies itself" to them. Legal argument with the facts of the case means restating them so that the case appears in a different part of the field than it did initially.

Remember that my objective is to make my lie-in look like a case plausibly covered by the rule permitting speech-type interferences with the m.o.p., rather than like a case clearly governed by the rule of no interferences with the m.o.p. Suppose that a mass picketing case has already gone against the workers. My first impression is that the lie-in is "even worse" from an interference point of view, and simultaneously "weaker" as a speech case. I will try to restate the facts of the mass picketing case to make it reappear in the field as more of an interference than the lie-in, and as less plausibly a case of protected speech.

I will do this by emphasizing that, in the mass picketing case, the court found that the workers were trying to physically prevent substitute workers from entering the plant, and that the situation was always on the verge of violence. I will de-emphasize the opinion's references to the signs and shouted slogans of the mass picket. By contrast, I will argue that the workers in the lie-in submitted peacefully to arrest, and could never have physically prevented passage of the buses by lying in front of them.

My hope is that you will eventually perceive the two cases as located in just the opposite position from that you saw them in initially, so that I can draw the boundary between rather than around them. Mass picketing will then fall on the side of interference, the lie-in on the side of speech.

✧　✧　✧

Changing the position of a precedent in the field is, as I've been describing it, analogous to changing the position of the case before us—the lie-in. But the analogy is misleading to the extent that the precedent, unlike the lie-in, comes already equipped with a holding. This complicates matters considerably.

If the facts of the precedent are on the boundary, then its holding is *part of* the boundary. The holding is a rule, or at least a little sub-rule, defining, in the abstract manner of any rule, a range of cases beyond this particular instance of mass picketing. These cases "in the vicinity" or "close to on point," along with any future fact situation that might be "on all fours" with it, are "settled" by the precedent. In other words, the holding of a case structures the field around the point represented by the fact situation of that case.

I must be able to restate the holding as well as the facts of the mass picketing case if I want to reposition my lie-in case with respect to the boundary. The work of restating the holding is closer to the work of restating the general rule than it is to that of repositioning a fact situation. For example, after I've restated the facts of the mass picketing case to emphasize forcible interferences with passage of substitute workers into the plant, I may want to restate the holding too. I will play down the original opinion's claim that because this was "action" it can receive First Amendment protection only if it was "unequivocally symbolic." I will claim that what the court prohibited was coercion of substitute workers, rather than an attempt at persuasion. This statement of the holding will make it easier to restate the general rule to include nonviolent civil disobedient lie-ins under the rubric of protected expression.

✧ ✧ ✧

We might think of the holding of the case as a line extending through the point represented by the facts. The line defines a set of cases that the holding has resolved one way or the other. When I redefine the holding, I inflect the line in some way, changing its direction so that it "covers" a different set of hypothetical situations.

Thus, when the mass picketing case becomes a case about "coercion vs. persuasion," it helps define the boundary between forbidden and permitted union activity differently than it did when it was about how "action" is unprotected unless "unequivocally symbolic."

The inflection of the line is desirable because, once I have done it, I won't have to spend a lot of time explaining how the lie-in is "unequivocally symbolic." I can admit that it is "action." My (much easier) argument will be that it is clearly persuasive rather than coercive action. Further, my new holding for the mass picketing case makes a nice little piece of the new boundary I am drawing between First Amendment cases and interference-with-property-rights cases. Mass picketing is not closely analogous to nonviolent civil disobedience, now that we've identified it as problematic because "coercive." So there is no inconsistency in forbidding it while tolerating lie-ins.

✧   ✧   ✧

Extending the field analogy yet a step further, we can use it to incorporate the "broadening" and "narrowing" of holdings into our analysis. Narrowing the holding, by restating it as a rule that depends for its application on many potentially idiosyncratic details of the particular case, is a shortening of the line that extends through the fact situation in the field. It means that there will be fewer hypothetical fact situations "covered" by the holding, and the case will therefore have less structuring effect on the field around it. Broadening is the opposite maneuver.

✧   ✧   ✧

Policies as forces in the field

Policy arguments are reasons for adopting a particular holding or mini-rule. They are aimed more specifically than philosophical or social theoretical justifications of whole systems and more abstractly than appeals to the raw equities immanent in "the facts." Policy argument is "second order" in relation to rule application or argument from precedent. It presupposes conscious choice about how the structure of the field should look, as opposed to simple subsumption of the facts to a norm that I grasp non-reflectively as part of a gestalt.

The arguer can pick and choose from a truly enormous repertoire of typical policy arguments and modify what he finds to fit the case at hand. The arguments come in matched contrary pairs, like certainty vs. flexibility, security vs. freedom of action, property as incentive to labor vs. property as incipient monopoly, no liability without fault vs. as between two innocents he who caused the damage should pay, the supremacy clause vs. local initiative, and so on.

A policy is not invalidated just because I ignore it in a case where it arguably applies. Our rough notion is that the two sides of the matched pair "differ in strength" from case to case. We might see the property-as-incentive-to-labor argument as very strong if the issue is whether there should be any private rights at all in mechanisms of interstate commerce, but as quite weak if the question is whether there should be a right to prevent peaceful individual picketing of an interstate bus company involved in a labor dispute.

The moment when I switch from one of the matched pairs to the other in response to a change in the fact situation can be quite dramatic. In this case, I might firmly believe that the interests in security and peaceful access to public spaces strongly support state law criminal sanctions against the lie-in. I might then turn around and argue against a federal injunction of the lie-in, on the ground that people should have a right to nonviolent civil disobedient protest, even if it inconveniences the public and the employer, and that repressive measures will make violence more rather than less likely.

✧ ✧ ✧

In a typical legal argument, policies are elaborated and strongly asserted without regard to their matched pairs. When I argue for state law criminal penalties, I don't have to explain, either as judge or as advocate, the rational basis of my endorsement of "nip it in the bud" here, and my contrary endorsement of "repression breeds violence" when we get to the injunction. In a sense, then, the practice of legal arguers (lawyers, judges, treatise writers) is endlessly contradictory. I assert my policy as "valid" and as "requiring" an outcome, and then blithely reject it, and, in the next case, endorse its exactly matching opposite, without giving any meta-level explanation of what keys me into one side or the other.

From the inside, however, I know from the beginning that this is just "the way we do" legal argument. I don't take the surface claim that the policy is "valid" and "requires" the outcome seriously at all. I work from a model of the opposing policies as forces or vectors, each of which has some "pull" on any given fact situation. They *seem* logically contradictory (how can I believe, at the same time. that "there should be no liability without fault," and that "as between two innocents he who caused the damage should pay") or so indeterminate that they can serve only as after-the-fact rationalizations of decisions reached on other grounds (who knows whether the injunction will "nip violence in the bud" or "just drive it underground and make it worse"?). But there is a sense in which both policies are valid at the same time, in every case. The question is which one turns out to be "stronger," or to weigh more in a "balancing test" applied to these particular facts, rather than which is correct in the abstract.

We can represent the process of arranging cases in a field, and the process of fixing a boundary between permitted and forbidden acts, in terms of this imagery of vectors and balancing. For example, the imaginary mass picketing and individual picketing cases discussed earlier had fact situations and holdings, but they also "involved" or "implicated" various policies. The mass picketing case implicated the general social policy in favor of political association and the general social policy against the use of force to resolve disputes. (Each case implicates as many policies as I can plausibly think up. Those mentioned here are illustrative, not exhaustive.)

Suppose we see the lie-in, in relation to mass picketing, as a "better" First Amendment case, and as a less serious interference with the employer's use of the m.o.p. during a strike. The "second order" interpretation of this intuitive ordering is that pro-speech policies apply more strongly, and pro-property policies less strongly, than in the mass picketing case. As we move from fact situation to fact situation across the field, the speech policy gets weaker, and the property policy stronger, until at the boundary they are in equilibrium. At this point a very small change in the relative forces of the policies produces a dramatic change in result. We "draw the line" and treat cases beyond the line repressively.

What this means is that we have to add to our model of the field of law the notion that, at every point in the field, contradictory policies exert different levels of force. Boundary lines in the field represent points of equilibrium of opposing forces. At points not on boundaries, one or another set of policies predominates. The policies are to be understood as gradients; they are strongest in the "core," where a given general rule seems utterly obvious in its application and also utterly "appropriate as a matter of social policy." The argument-set supporting the general rule diminishes in force as we move from the core outward toward the periphery, and ultimately to a boundary with another general rule.

The boundary appears to me as "there" in three quite different ways. First, it is a line, a rule that was implicit in the statement of the general rule. For example, I may see the idea that there shall be no laws against "free speech" as implicitly including nonverbal expression. Second, the boundary is a line running through all the limiting cases. Suppose that individual but not mass picketing is all right; that threats of non-association with substitute workers but not threats to call demand notes are all right. The boundary "connects the dots." Third, as we have just seen, the boundary is like the line in a magnetic field formed by iron filings exactly balanced between two distant magnets. State law criminal penalties against a lie-in are desirable and don't violate the first amendment, but the addition of a federal injunction is undesirable and would be unconstitutional, say, because the injunction is just a little bit "too much."

We have already discussed legal argument as the restatement of general rules and the re-selection of facts so that a case that initially appeared "covered" by rule A turns out to be covered by rule B. And we have discussed the manipulation of the facts and holdings of precedents to redefine the boundary. My goal in policy argument is analogous. First, I develop a potential holding for my lie-in case, such as that there shall be no federal injunction of nonviolent civil disobedient protests in labor disputes. Then I develop some policy arguments as to why this rule is preferable to an alternative (usually a straw man) or to the rule proposed by the employer. For example, I argue that if the workers feel strongly enough to undergo arrest and criminal charges, they almost certainly feel strongly enough to do something violent if they are not permitted their symbolic protest. It follows that, far from "nipping violence in the bud," an injunction will likely lead to unorganized individual acts of violence, such as shooting out bus tires on the open highway.

But this argument is unlikely to be enough. Once I have taken the step into the "second order," forsaking the strategy of mere rule application, I evoke in the mind of my audience the whole force field of this area of law. I will now have to take steps to preserve the coherence of the overall policy "picture." This means restating policy arguments in other decided cases. For example, suppose that in the mass picketing case the court justified a prohibitory rule on the ground that unless you nip violence in the bud it develops until it is unstoppable.

My problem is that in the lie-in case I am arguing that worker anger makes it important to tolerate civil disobedience, and this position seems inconsistent with a "nipping in the bud" strategy against mass picketing. In order to restore order to the field, I will "distinguish" the mass picketing case as follows. Mass picketing is essentially uncontrollable and naturally tends to escalate toward violence. In the civil disobedience case, by contrast, the police exercise detailed and intense control. Though the initial emotion may be greater in the lie-in, the setting allows the release of emotion without escalation. Since the situation is already under control but still serving to release emotion, an injunction is likely to be counterproductive overkill.

[Let me remind the patient reader that I have no idea whether the preceding policy arguments and distinctions are "any good," that is, whether they would be persuasive to a person a little knowledgeable in the field. One begins the work of legal argument enveloped in ignorance of what the law "is" and with little sense of what may be the conventional wisdom about how the law works in practice. I will find out about these matters by doing research and by asking people. In consequence, I'll flatly abandon some arguments while I develop others. What I am trying to do here is describe what the work process in its initial stages feels like from the inside.]

✧ ✧ ✧

Rules vs. Standards

The boundary can be cast either as a rule (a determinate outcome on easily determined facts) or as a standard (ad hoc judgment required) applying a value, like good faith or reasonableness, or an abstraction, like foreseeability or promotion of competition. When the boundary is cast as a standard, the argument that a particular fact situation falls within it will often look a lot like policy argument—may indeed merge by degrees into it. There are "formal" arguments for rules and for standards, and against rules and against standards. These are policy arguments about the appropriateness of using a rule or a standard in the particular case.

✧ ✧ ✧

Social and historical stereotypes

These are part of the stock in trade of legal argument. By a social stereotype, I mean, for example, the raw image of "worker blocks bus"—an unshaven large burly white man without a tie or jacket aggressively obstructing innocent third-party passengers (us!) who have to sit passively until someone comes to their aid. I might reverse the stereotype by expanding the time frame of the story, a la Kelman, and adding lots of facts, until we get "bus monopoly's intransigence finally breaks patience of Job-like toilers." Historical stereotypes are ideas like "the nineteenth century was a time of agrarian individualism so it was natural for people then to accept the doctrine of *caveat emptor*."

✧   ✧   ✧

Overruling

If policy argument is second order in relation to mere rule application, overruling is third order. Without question there are *some* circumstances in which, as a federal district court judge, I can redraw the boundary between permitted and forbidden conduct without restating the facts of cases, so that cases find themselves looking at a boundary where once they were looking at home, and looking at home across an open space where once there was a boundary.

There are maxims about overruling. The district court, a trial court, should be less quick to do it than an appeals court. It is more permissible to overrule a doctrine riddled with exceptions, and consequently more honored in the breach than in the observance, than to overrule a vital modern doctrine that dominates its field like a young Mars. And so forth. There are cases in which a course of law reform has become the norm, so that *not to* overrule a case would appear an abuse of discretion. (Suppose that the Supreme Court had upheld separate-but-equal public playground facilities after desegregating schools, public accommodations, government offices.)

When I first began thinking about this subject, the possibility of overruling seemed a dramatically important aspect of the judicial activist's situation. Indeed, it seemed to mean that there is no such thing as a conflict between "the law" and how-I-want-to-come-out, since I can change the law by over-ruling to make it correspond to my heart's desire. On further reflection, this has come to seem a shallow view.

First, though overruling is a third order practice, it is nonetheless subject to the calculus of legitimacy I have been describing. I can't overrule with impunity any more than I can disturb the field with impunity in any other way. The set of maxims by which the overruling decision will be judged are pretty vague, but if the decision isn't convincing, I will find myself less able to persuade the next time around and feeling guilty about violating role constraints.

Second, my power to overrule, seen as a kind of ultimate power to reorder the field, is counterbalanced by the notion of legislative supremacy. I can't "overrule" a statute. *But* the statute may be trumped by the state and federal constitutions, of which I am interpreter here. *But* though I can use the constitutions to overrule the statute, I have no power to overrule the constitutions themselves. *But* even this is not the end of the story, since the constitutions don't seem, a priori, to be any more conceivably self-applying than any other set of legal norms. Many great cases branch down from the sacred texts, and these I *can* overrule.

The upshot of these twists and turns is that I decide about overruling enmeshed in the field of law, subject to its typical constraint that I argue persuasively across some perceived obviousness gap, or forfeit my charismatic power and get reversed on appeal into the bargain. It is an added power; it enhances my freedom to make the law correspond to how-I-want-to-come-out beyond what it would be if I had always to work in the first order of rule application or the second order of policy argument. But it liberates me as a technological innovation might liberate a worker in a medium—as, say, the invention of new casting techniques changes the possibilities of sculpture. New techniques bring new constraints along with new possibilities. They change as well as reducing the experience of constraint. It becomes harder than it was before to say with authority what can and cannot be done in the medium. But the overruling option does not make the judge all-powerful.

✧   ✧   ✧

Typical field configurations

As I initially apprehend it, a legal field is more than just a collection of general rules, boundaries, precedents, and vectors. I will almost certainly experience it as patterned, as a field with a particular configuration. Of course each field is different from every other one. But in the gestalt process by which we grasp it, we employ—albeit non-reflectively—what we might call "configuration-types." We get a cognitive grip on the particularity of a given field by relating it to one or more of these types, distorting it in the process.

We can loosely array configuration-types according to how impacted they are. By this I mean that some fields seem to offer more opportunities for one kind or another of legal argument than others. Here are my candidates, beginning with the type that seems to offer least opportunity for overcoming whatever the initial distance may have been between the law and how-I-want-to-come-out.

The impacted field

In the impacted field boundaries are long straight lines, meaning that there are general rules determining the limits of general rules. For example, we might have a rule that "protected speech," must be either speech or the dissemination of written texts. The "further we go" without making exceptions (e.g., we uphold censorship of a dance performance with obvious political content, or of a mime show) the longer the straight boundary line. In the impacted field, there are a substantial number of cases distributed in a regular pattern along the boundary, dispelling any doubt that the rule means what it says. The dance and mime cases have actually been decided.

Moreover, the courts deciding them did so with holdings that carefully incorporated the cases under the most general statement of the general rule, in the process reaffirming all the earlier cases along the line, while predicting that at points in between the decided cases the courts would adhere to the existing pattern. Behind the lines, there is a nice scatter pattern of easy cases, and they get easier and easier as you approach the core, all in accord with the gradient hypothesis about social policies. This pattern makes it hard to imagine "parachuting in," so to speak, with a surprise case permitting peacetime national security censorship of a newspaper editorial criticizing the government.

When I apprehend the field as impacted, I apprehend it as hard to manipulate. Those long straight boundaries, reinforced at regular intervals with precedents whose holdings exactly track the line, will defy the arts I have been describing. My initial sense will be that, unless I can do my work on the facts of the lie-in itself, I am going to be in trouble. But remember that we are not speaking of actual, objective properties of the field, but rather of my initial apprehension of it.

When I set to work, for example, at reading a lot of those cases I vaguely remember, everything may change. I haven't yet tried to restate the rules and cases and policies in a serious way. My initial impression, that the field is impacted, is as much a *product* of my initial fear that I won't be able to come up with a viable legal argument for the lie-in as it is a *cause* of that fear. If you wait a minute, the field may suddenly look a lot different, as happened above when I finally began to see a way to tuck the lie-in under the wing of the First Amendment.

The case of first impression

Sometimes the field presents itself as structured everywhere except in the vicinity of the case at hand. The boundary line is vague throughout the area of the lie-in; no precedents appear nearby; and, significantly, the policy vectors seem to be of about equal force, not just along a thin line of equilibrium, but throughout the border region. If the vectors are about equal and also relatively very strong, it is not just a case of first impression, but a "great" case. If the vectors are weak, then it is the routine case of penny-ante judicial creativity.

If the field has this structure, but the lie-in seems to fall outside the area of indeterminacy, a basic argumentative tactic is to restate the facts to put it there. This changes the situation from an adverse one, in which rule application seems to settle things against me, to a neutral one, in which everyone will concede that there are good legal arguments on both sides, and the whole proceeding has the air of a solemn sports event.

The impacted field and the case of first impression represent constraint and freedom as they are conceived within the legal tradition itself. The case of first impression does not threaten that tradition because the freedom involved is, first, exceptional, and, second, freedom constrained by its narrow context. The case is a kind of clearing of freedom in the endless forest of constraint. Because we exercise freedom where there is no constraint, it doesn't threaten constraint. Moreover, the judge's action fills in a part of the clearing, so that the freedom of cases of first impression can be understood as self-annihilating. The more times judges exercise this freedom the less of it there will be, as the boundaries get staked out case by case.

The following configuration-types differ from both the impacted field and the case of first impression because of their ambiguity. Rather than presenting themselves either as hopeless (constraint) or as open (freedom), they present themselves as opportunities whose ultimate meaning we will fix through the work of argument.

✧   ✧   ✧

The unrationalized field

Imagine that there are lots and lots of cases in the general vicinity of the boundary, some coming out for the workers and some for the employer. But they are decided "on their facts," with minimal argumentation and narrow or conclusory or obviously logically defective holdings. Just because there are so many cases clustered around the boundary, there are many, many occasions for rearrangement by restatement of facts. This will be especially true where there are lots of details available for each precedent (so the restater has free play in selection) or almost no details at all (so the restater can dismiss the case as ambiguous). A field of this kind invites an opinion proposing a new rule and showing how all the old cases, properly understood, are consistent with it. Because the earlier cases are unrationalized but numerous, the exercise may be particularly convincing as "order out of chaos," and a great relief to the audience. Or it may fail miserably, leaving things more disorderly than they were before.

✧　✧　✧

The contradictory field

This is the situation in which there are lots of cases on both sides, but the company has won some that seriously impair free speech, and the workers have won some that seriously impair employer control of the m.o.p. during a strike. The courts have prohibited all picketing, say, but have permitted unlimited secondary boycott activity.

In a situation like this, connecting the dots so as to draw the boundary requires a zig-zag line that cuts deep first into one territory and then into the other. Each opinion fully restates the policy vectors so that it looks as though the outcome is "required." But the result is that a given policy appears to vary widely in force at points that are near each other in the field.

These rapid fluctuations along a contorted boundary suggest that "something is wrong." The boundary between strict liability and negligence in the law of unintentional tort has much this quality. Cases that openly impose strict liability are only part of the picture (though, as every law student knows, it is hard to decide what is an "ultrahazardous" activity, given the precedents and the ambiguous definition). There are also so-called "historical" instances, as with animals and nuisance. There are situations such as res ipsa loquitur and the manipulation of informed consent in which the courts impose de facto strict liability behind a screen of fault rhetoric. And courts interpret the reasonable person standard to permit liability without fault, right next to cases in which they "individualize" the standard to prevent that outcome.

There are lots of arguments for strict liability and lots of arguments for the fault standard in these cases. The problem is that if one took the arguments in any of the cases seriously, one would have to overrule dozens and dozens of cases based on the opposed policy in the matching pair. Consequently, almost any case can appear to be of first impression, since virtually all cases seem to fall midway between cases decided for strict liability and cases decided for the fault standard. Instead of a field divided in half by a straight line that represents an equilibrium of forces, we have an extremely complex structure shot through with interstices. There really is no boundary. Every point not occupied by a recent precedent is contestable.

✧   ✧   ✧

The collapsed field

A field collapses, in this lingo, when the policy arguments on one side of the boundary get restated so as to abolish the boundary. One of the contending general rules then appears correctly applicable across the field so as to obliterate the counter-rule.

Collapse is usually an event quickly recognized to threaten the whole enterprise, so the collapsing argument is not just "accepted."

Rather it is there as a possible, plausibly legal, incontestably legitimate and sometimes highly persuasive argument *in every single case.* On the other side are ad hoc appeals to factual peculiarities, arguments harking back shamelessly to a more innocent time, mistakes, intuitionistic protests against collapse, but no coherent argument for a line that would hold against the collapsing argument.

In *Shelley v. Kraemer,* if enforcement of discriminatory covenants is state action, then the private sphere "disappears," since all private arrangements are dependent for their structure on enforcement of private law ground rules. In *Wickard v. Fillburn,* if wheat grown for your own consumption affects interstate commerce by reducing demand, then it is hard to see what activity can ever be "intrastate." In *Pennsylvania Coal v. Mahon,* Holmes points out that all police power regulations "take property" in the sense of impoverishing someone, but proposes to solve the problem only by an incoherent test of "how much taking." In *Hoffman v. Red Owl Stores* and *Drennan v. Star Paving,* the court allows a promissory estoppel recovery where there was no gratuitous promise and indeed no consideration problem of any kind. There was merely a failure to comply with the formalities that indicate intent to make the promise binding. If promissory estoppel applies in such cases, it potentially abolishes formalities in any case where there was reliance.

✧   ✧   ✧

The loopified field

The notion of loopification makes people uptight, and since it's not that important here, I'll just mention it briefly. We apprehend the field as loopified when supposedly easy cases in the heartlands of the territories of the opposing rules seem closer together (around the back, so to speak) than cases that are opposite one another along the boundary.

For example, the intimate relations of family members are simultaneously those that seem most clearly private (e.g., as described in *Griswold v. Connecticut* or *Roe v. Wade)* and those that, because of their implications for the public weal, are subject to the most intense and intrusive state regulation (as in the standardless determination of child custody in the "best interests of the child"). Or take promissory estoppel, which now applies most typically to a business transaction in which there has been a failure to comply with formalities and in which the measure of damages may actually be the expectancy. This core promissory estoppel case is hard to distinguish from the core case in which, according to the traditional wisdom of, e.g., *Baird v. Gimbel,* the doctrine simply has no applicability at all.

✧ ✧ ◇

I hope, as I begin research on the lie-in case, that the field will present itself in a somewhat disordered configuration—as unrationalized, for example—and I fear that I will confront an impacted field, with my case firmly planted behind "enemy lines." One goal of legal argument is to recast the field so that it will end up looking impacted, but with the lie-in case now securely where it ought to be.

If the field looked well ordered for me initially but at the end of the argument the field looks contradictory, I have lost ground, even if I am still quite plausibly presenting the lie-in case as one that has to be resolved for the workers. On the other hand, if I begin with an unfavorable impacted field and end up with a plausible case of first impression, or a plausible case in a loopified field, I have done quite well.

The reason you want to end up with an impacted field (with your case favorably placed) is that the impacted field's orderly boundaries, its neatly disposed precedents, with their congruent holdings and smooth policy gradients, is the very image of legal necessity. If you persuade your audience that the field is like this, the audience will see the decision-making process as a simple exercise in rule application. The case will "decide itself."

By contrast, a case in a contradictory field, no matter how plausibly presented, can't seem necessarily to come out your way. The chaotic configuration of the contradictory field—no matter where you are in the field there are cases all around that come out all different ways—is a symbolic representation of contingency dressed up to look like necessity. This may be a relief, given how bad things looked to start with, but it's never the ideal end of the argument about this case.

✧　✧　✧

Remember, though, that this case is not the whole story. In my role as a liberal activist judge, I have long term goals with respect to the configuration of the various fields I work in. For example, suppose that I can decide the lie-in case for the workers if I emphasize one aspect of the facts but in the process will reinforce a boundary in the field that I see as congealed injustice. My goal of law reform may be to collapse that boundary—say by establishing that there is no a priori distinction between worker rights in the m.o.p. and ownership rights—so that the concept of ownership cannot define a core of employer prerogative that must remain immune from worker meddling during a strike.

I may be willing to sacrifice something in the way of total convincingness in this particular lie-in case in order to disorder the field. Maybe I will emphasize the extent to which the holding of my lie-in case conflicts with holdings in the long string of picketing cases, so as to create a consciousness of discontinuity that will induce workers and their lawyers to expand the lie-in into a deep salient extending toward the core of the employer's property rights.

✧　✧　✧

Just as I have multiple objectives in constructing my argument, I have multiple materials and a variety of different kinds of moves I can make with each element in the field. As I set about the task of argument, these possibilities generate a rough sense of an *economy of the field*. By this I mean that there are systems of trade-offs between desired objectives and between the different kinds of moves I can make with the materials available to me. For example, I just described a possible trade-off between making the most convincing possible argument against an injunction in this particular case and my long-term goal of destabilizing the rule that the workers can't interfere with the owner's use of the m.o.p. during a strike. Trade-offs at the level of goals are executed through decisions about which elements in the field to manipulate and how much. These are *strategies of execution* of a given field manipulation.

A strategy is a set of choices between, say, distinguishing a given case by restating its facts and distinguishing the same case by restating its holding. Or between distinguishing all picketing cases from the lie-in on the basis that the lie-in is civil disobedience, and distinguishing the lie-in from mass picketing on the ground that it's non-coercive, while emphasizing its similarity to individual picketing.

The notion is that there is a rough relationship of substitution between different manipulative moves. I have a choice between dramatically redrawing a boundary and dramatically restating the facts of cases so that they appear on the other side of an unmoved boundary. Moreover, choices between moves in one part of the field—or with respect to one element, say, precedents—influence and indeed constrain the choices that are available in other parts of the field.

I have been developing through the preceding discussion a particular strategy for arguing against an injunction of the lie-in. Some elements of the strategy are: the choice of a First Amendment general defense of the action; the choice not to attack state law civil and criminal penalties short of injunction; the choice to distinguish mass picketing cases as coercive rather than as "not speech," and so on. It seems obvious to me that there must be other possible strategies, though for the moment the only one that comes to mind is that of using the Wagner Anti-injunction Act.

One of the effects of adopting a strategy is a kind of tunnel vision: one is inside the strategy, sensitive to its internal economy, its history of trade-offs, attuned to developing it further but at least temporarily unable to imagine any other way to go.

But a strategy is also a *practical commitment.* Because it hangs together, the strategy imposes multiple constraints on how I respond to any new aspect of the case. It's not just a matter of logical consistency: the strategy has a tone and a style. For example, hard-nosed nip-it-in-the-bud rhetoric about mass picketing will be in tension with repression-just-makes-it-worse rhetoric in the lie-in, even though there is no logical problem. Moreover, a strategy is an investment of time. Once I've put in the work of developing its many interlocking parts, it will cost me plenty if I respond to a new question with an answer that would force revision of everything that's gone before.

In legal argument as in other production processes, practitioners have an intuitive idea of efficiency in the deployment of the available materials. Anyone who has done legal argument knows what it means to do it "neatly" or "elegantly," meaning at a minimum expenditure of ... something. A part of this complex notion is that if you are mainly interested in who wins the particular case, you should persuade us that the lie-in is non-enjoinable with the least possible restatement of the facts and holdings of other cases, the least possible rearrangement of policy vectors, and the least possible movement of the boundary between free speech and interference with property. If, by contrast, you want to "make some law," you should do that, too, so as to accomplish the greatest possible movement of the boundary with the least possible disturbance of the other elements of the field.

A kind of quotient notion emerges. Success at the skill of legal argument can be measured by how little you disturb the field in order to persuasively achieve a given restructuring, whether it's a big restructuring through law making or a small one by making sure the good guys win this case. It's the ratio rather than the absolute amount of movement or of disturbance that counts.

✧   ✧   ✧

My uncertainty about whether I will succeed in making a convincing argument

Up to now I have presented the activity of argument as a kind of work, undertaken in a medium, with a purpose. The purpose was to convince the audience that, contrary to our initial impression, a decision denying an injunction in the lie-in is in accord with the law. I undertake this argumentative labor with a number of ulterior motives, such as avoiding reversal on appeal, fulfilling my obligation to the public, and so forth. I hope that by developing a convincing argument against the injunction I will avoid a loss of credibility as a judge (indeed, I hope to increase my credibility through a strong opinion).

There is an ideal scenario in which I am able to represent the legal field so that the law corresponds exactly to how-I-want-to-come-out. What was initially an impacted field with the lie-in unequivocally prohibited (an easy case) becomes, to the surprise of my public, an impacted field in which the lie-in is a case that is clearly permitted (or at least not enjoinable). I close a large obviousness gap by a field manipulation that is notably elegant—a dramatic change in outcome with surprisingly little disturbance of the elements of the field.

When my reasoning turns out this way, I feel euphoria, indeed a moment of dangerous omnipotence, delight at the plasticity of the natural/social field-medium, and narcissistic ecstasy at the favorable reaction of my public (not to speak of sober joy at all the good I will be able to do with my increased credibility). But before you put me down as an egotist, I want to add that some element of this pleasure is quite legitimate. I had an intuition about the justice of

the situation—how-I-wanted-to-come-out in this case was in accord with an intuition that the law as I initially apprehended it was
unfair to a particular group. If I have succeeded in making the law
fairer to that group, my pleasure will be in part an altruistic emotion that seems to me no cause for shame: I will have helped out.
Too bad it doesn't always turn out that way.

I will describe below some of the ways things don't turn out
ideally. But first dwell for a bit on my uncertainty, as I begin my
argument, about what will happen during its course. I have an
initial estimate, a guess about how large the obviousness gap is,
about the resources I will have to marshal in order to overcome it,
and about the chances that I will fall short to one degree or another.
But why can't I tell in advance the more or less precise dimensions
of my problem, the means at my disposal, and the quality of my solution? I don't know *why*. But here is *how* I don't know in advance.

✧   ✧   ✧

Projection

I may have misjudged the way the field will look to other people.
I'm trying to persuade not only myself but also some hypothetical
public. But I have to construct their way of seeing it on the basis
of my own vision. It often happens that the field looks to me at
first glance at least unrationalized and very possibly contradictory,
while others see it as at least close to impacted. In other words, I
know I have a bias, measured by the vision of others, toward seeing the field as undetermined, as unstructured, as open to all kinds
of manipulation. Remember that my initial apprehension of the
configuration of the field is a gestalt process, very firmly located in
the eye of the beholder, yet dependent on stimuli that are external.
Other people seem to me to see the field as always impacted, and
adversely at that, until they have put an inordinate amount of pain
into loosening it up.

Virtu

The skill of legal argument is to close a big obviousness gap with minimal disturbance of the elements of the field. It is the skill of combining the different moves—restating facts and holdings and rules and policies and stereotypes—in such a way as to achieve multiple goals at minimal cost.

There is no way to be sure you will be able to do this the next time you try. How much you can change the field through argument is a property of *yours*. That is, it is determined by your skill, as well as a property of the field, but the property of yours is unknowable in advance. There is such a thing as a good day and such a thing as a bad day. Internal psychic factors like adrenalin, panic, fatigue, but also internal factors that seem random, or psychoanalytically knowable after the fact, all impinge. Life is a gamble, here as everywhere else.

Hidden properties

My initial apprehension of the field doesn't tell me that much about it. An analogy is my initial apprehension of a body of water through which I am going to navigate a boat. I can see the surface of the water but usually not what lies beneath it. Yet lots and lots of signs on the surface indicate what is beneath. Some people are terrific at "reading" the surface; others not so good. But no matter how good you are at reading, there is lots that just isn't knowable in advance. In legal argument, I have no way of knowing with any precision what is contained in the hundreds of cases I haven't read that might be relevant to my problem, or in the thousands of other legal materials scattered across creation waiting to be put to use here.

✧　✧　✧

The consequence of these different kinds of uncertainty is that I can never know in advance whether it will be possible to develop a legal argument for how-I-want-to-come-out that will persuade any part of my audience. Sometimes, the problems are obvious from the start. I never break through my initial panicked sense that this is a case the workers can't possibly win. It sometimes happens that my sense that they can't possibly win emerges slowly as I pursue what at first seemed like a promising course of argument.

Sometimes it's less dramatic than running up against the brick wall of the experienced objectivity of the rule. Maybe it turns out that I can make an argument that is "plausible" but won't actually convince many people; or that I can convince my audience that the law is a lot more favorable to the workers than they thought, but not so favorable as to prohibit an injunction of this particular illegal action. I may come up with a field-manipulation that strikes me as clumsy or just plain wrong—one that wouldn't convince me for a minute of anything—but which I think will appeal to this public as highly plausible.

I experience the course of events as contingent. I don't have, and I know I don't have, a technique for predicting with a high degree of certainty what will happen to my first impression of conflict between the law and how-I-want-to-come-out. I can only find out the actual posture of the law by going through the work of argument. While it's happening, the situation seems to open toward a multiplicity of possible outcomes, none of which would violate any strongly held theoretical tenets.

✧   ✧   ✧

When I've finished, I may be able to represent what happened as the necessary consequence of the "state of the law" when I began. But I won't really know why it turned out the way it did. In particular, if I fail to develop a plausible legal argument against an injunction of the lie-in, I won't know whether the reason was that I lacked skill in manipulating the field or that the "inherent properties of the field" were such that there was nothing I could have done. Did I screw up, or was I doomed from the start?

I am not in a condition of total ignorance about the failure. Next week another judge or lawyer may produce an argument against enjoining the lie-in that is highly plausible, and dissolves the felt objectivity of the rule, at least as applied to this case. If that happens, I will say to myself, with a lot of confidence, that my failure last week was a failure of skill rather than something preordained by the latent structure of the field. Or I may discover a whole series of earlier unsuccessful attempts to argue the case convincingly and conclude that my failure was not so shameful after all.

Knowledge of this kind is consistent with the sense of radical contingency I am asserting here. When someone else does what I couldn't do I learn that my failure was a failure of skill; and there is suggestive evidence in the failure of others that my failure was a consequence of the properties of the field. But it isn't possible to prove convincingly that there was just no way to make it fly. You can't prove it can't be done.

I have had many times the initial apprehension of the objective coverage of a case by a rule. I have many times started out thinking, "no way." And I have had many times the experience of apparent objectivity dissolving under the pressure of the work of legal argument. I have no theory that tells me in advance when that will happen and when it won't. I just have to try and see. When it doesn't work, sometimes someone else can do it. And sometimes I come back to the problem later and succeed where before I seemed to fail through no fault of my own. *From the inside,* what happens to my initial experience of the rule as objective is radically contingent.

I can imagine what it would be like to be able to tell in advance whether or not the rule's objective self-application will stand the test of time and effort. I can imagine having a technique, like the technique of a surveyor, say, that would tell me with great confidence that if I extend a bridge's span at a particular angle in a particular direction it will eventually hit the other side of the ravine at a predetermined spot. But that's just not the way it is in legal argument, at least for me. And in all honesty I have to say that people who think differently have, in my experience, turned out not to know what they are talking about.

✧   ✧   ✧

[*The quantitative question*. It seems irresistible to ask at this point some such question as, "How often will the field be impacted or otherwise unbudgeable through legal argument?" If this is a question about the experience of a particular judge or group of judges, then it is at least intelligible. We could devise an empirical investigation into that experience, perhaps through interviews about past cases. We could even attempt an historical inquiry, based on more diffuse and suggestive data, into how the experience of judging has changed through time. Some of my own work is in this mode. I would venture the hypothesis that experiences of the manipulability of the field have become steadily more common in American history since 1776.

But I don't think the question is usually asked with this kind of answer in mind. It is a question about the *nature* of the field, about an objective property of the legal materials in use in a society at a particular moment in its history. That there can be no answer to the question posed in this way seems to me implicit in what I have already said.

The field is unknowable except through experience, and there is no "value neutral" perspective from which we can assess the "correctness" of a report of immovability. Whether judges have the experience may vary with how hard and how often they try to manipulate the field when it initially appears impacted. It may vary with the critical techniques available in their legal culture to dissolve the initial appearance of objectivity. It may change according to the quantity and the particular quality of the flow of cases they adjudicate, and according to whether they must habitually consider cases from many autonomous jurisdictions.

It is probably overdetermined by all of these things at once, and by many other aspects of judicial reality as well. One of these aspects is probably the extent to which judges learn in law school to anticipate that socially constructed systems of meaning, and particularly law fields, will be open to multiple interpretations. If we decided to "count" experiences of objectivity, we would have to decide what counts as an instance. But there just isn't any "natural" set of assumptions, any model of the "juge moyen sensuel" to use as a standard in determining what particular law fields are "really" like. The quantitative question is simply unanswerable.

What then can be said of the body of legal materials "itself," considered in isolation from the particular contexts within which particular judges experience it? Not much. We have no reason to believe that the field is *ever* unbudgeable otherwise than as a consequence of the failure of particular judges to find a way to budge it. But we cannot assert the contrary either: it *may* be true that a given field was experienced as immovable because it *was* immovable, and that's all there was to it.]

✧   ✧   ✧

The normative power of the field

Throughout the discussion to this point, I have spoken as a judge who knows how he wants to come out and is vigorously trying to bring the law into accord. Sometimes I apprehend the law as plastic and cooperative, sometimes as resistant or even adamant, but me and my favored outcome are always the same. It is now time to critique the how-I-want-to-come-out pole of our duality. First, however, let's reify it with an acronym: HIWTCO.

HIWTCO is not a datum given externally, something that comes into the picture from outside. HIWTCO is *relative to the field*. This is true in the weak sense that I have decided HIWTCO in response to a question posed in terms of the existing social universe that includes law. I don't want these particular workers, living in our particular society under a particular set of legal rules to be enjoined from lying-in. I can't even formulate HIWTCO without referring to this legal context to give that result a meaning.

But HIWTCO is relative to the law field in a much more interesting and important way. I've been treating the law field as though it were a physical medium, clay or bricks, when what it is in fact is a set of declarations by other people (possibly including an earlier me) about how ethically serious people ought to respond to situations of conflict. As I manipulate the field, I am reading and rereading these declarations, apparently addressed to me, and trying to absorb their messages about what I ought to do. Indeed, before I ever heard of this case, I was already knowledgeable about hundreds of opinions by judges and lawyers and legislators about how to handle conflicts roughly analogous to this one.

As a preliminary matter this means that we are *not* dealing with a confrontation between "my gut feeling about the case" and the law, unless we understand my "gut" as an organ deeply conditioned by existence in our legalized universe. I simply don't have intuitions about social justice that are independent of my knowledge of what judges and legislators have done in the past about situations like the one before me. Other actors in the legal system have influenced, persuaded, outraged, puzzled, and instructed me, until I can never be sure in what sense an opinion I strongly hold is "really" mine rather than theirs. I don't even think such a question has an answer.

But the more important point is that my initial impression of conflict between the law and HIWTCO may disappear because HIWTCO changes, as well as because I manage to change the law. Further, the very resistance of the law to change in the direction of HIWTCO may impel HIWTCO to change in the direction of the law. I may find myself persuaded by my study of the materials that my initial apprehension of HIWTCO was wrong. I may find that I now want to come out the way I initially perceived the law coming out. This is what I mean by the normative power of the field.

✧ ✧ ✧

I try to move the law in the direction of HIWTCO, and to the extent the law is resistant, I find HIWTCO under pressure to move toward the law. But neither HIWTCO nor the law field are physical objects. If I experience "pressure" as I read through the legal materials, if the very fact of my initial apprehension that the law favors the employer exerts pressure, it is because the field is a message rather than a thing. It is a message of a kind I'm familiar with, a message of a kind I've dealt with before. Indeed, I am one of the authors of the message.

Precedents come to me as stories called fact situations that judges resolved in particular ways. What they did interests me in the way an earlier painter's work might interest a later painter. But interest is too weak a word. Especially when they are put together in patterns, precedents reveal possibilities that it would have taken me a long time to come up with, or that I might never have come up with at all. I look at six outcomes, and I say to myself, "Oh, they devised a strategy of banning all picketing, but allowing just about any kind of secondary boycott. Hmm. I wonder why. Oh, I get it, they had a rough distinction between physically confrontive and non-confrontive tactics. Or maybe they were concerned with workers' freedom not to contract in the boycott cases, and worried about the implications for business combinations if they banned labor combinations."

Just studying these patterns may change my view because the study will set my mind going in directions that it otherwise wouldn't have taken. But there is also the elemental normative power of any outcome reached by people I identify with. Because I think they were up to the same thing I am up to, *whatever* they came up with has in its favor my initial sense that it's probably what I would have come up with too.

I place my lie-in in the field among the various precedents, as more of an interference than, for example, individual picketing. Immediately, the analogical weight of the precedents pulls me toward wanting to come out as "the law" would have me come out. "Given what I know about what they were up to, by inference from the way they came out in those cases, I think they would have come out as follows in this case. If they would have come out that way, then I should come out that way too." This is the first order normative power of the field.

The second order normative power of the field comes from the fact that all these judges (and others) have left us more than just a record of fact situations and outcomes. They wrote opinions full of overtly normative explanations of outcomes by reference to rules and policies. There are hundreds of particular statements about *why* we should come out in a particular way under particular circumstances, sometimes very particularly defined circumstances, but sometimes how we should come out in large classes of fact situations quite abstractly defined (e.g., the workers can't interfere with the owner's use of the m.o.p. during a strike).

Now the practice of recording outcomes for fact situations, along with messages about why those outcomes are ethically and politically and legally correct, is no great mystery to me, since I do it all the time. I know first-hand what it means to try to indicate for the future how some future dispute should be resolved, and I have a good idea of what it is like to succeed. The person you've tried to influence says to you something like, "I had this problem, and I wondered what you would have to say about it, so I looked up your decision in the X case, where you gave your theory of what disruptive tactics labor should be permitted to use during a strike, and I found it very helpful. In fact, you might say what I did in the Y case was try to apply your theory. Of course, you may think I botched it completely."

I believe that it is possible to record messages about how to deal with future situations which will be intelligible to actors in the future, that it is possible for those actors to set out to "follow" the messages or directions, and that sometimes they do actually do something that is well described as "following the message." I sometimes feel that the people who set down all these messages that together make up the field had in mind something like the case before me and intended to instruct me to resolve it in a particular way. They are telling me not only that this is the rule they would apply, and here's how to apply it, but also that it is the *right* rule, that it is the way I ought to come out.

The second order normative power of the field comes from the fact that I identify with these ought-speakers. I respect them. I honor them. When they speak, I listen. I even tremble if I think I am going against their collective wisdom. They are members of the same community working on the same problems. They are *old;* they are *many.* They are steeped in a tradition of serious ethical inquiry whose power I have felt on countless occasions, a tradition that seems to me a partially valid great accomplishment of the often cruddy civilization of which I am a tiny part.

✧   ✧   ✧

It is no good telling me that my reverence for the messages of these ancients is "irrational." It's not a question of rationality. When I read their words, it is as though I myself were talking. (Of course, when I'm reading my own earlier opinions, it *is* me in an earlier incarnation who's talking.) I am not able to treat their ethical pronouncements about how to decide cases like this one as though they were a set of randomly generated possible answers to a math problem. In that case, I test each answer "coldly," so to speak, without any investment at all in its correctness or incorrectness. But as I sit reading the messages of the ancients about cases like this one (or even, I may sometimes feel with horror, about this very case neatly anticipated), I can't remain neutral. I want them to agree with me. And I want to agree with them. I feel I *ought* to agree with them.

In this state of mind, I may find myself adopting the voice of the ancients, knowing what they are talking about when they extol the sacredness of owner's rights and feeling that what they are saying accurately expresses something that I think too. I set out to manipulate the field so that the law would favor the lie-in, but in order to do that I have to enter into the discourse of law. In the process, I have to undergo its intimate prestige. I discover that I know what they were talking about because I myself am capable of thinking just what they thought. At that point, the normative force of the field is just one side in an interior discussion between my divided selves about who really should win this case anyway.

✧ ✧ ✧

Who is the field?

The messages that constitute the field are on one level just a set of verbal formulae. On another, they are speech I imaginatively impute to the "ancients." On a third level, the resistance of the field is another name for my ambivalence about whether or not I should enjoin the lie-in. To the question "who is the field," the answer has ultimately to be that the field is me, resisting myself.

✧ ✧ ✧

Conversion

It is possible that I will resolve my ambivalence by adopting the field as I initially apprehended it as a correct ethical statement as well as a correct perception of what the law is. In other words, I will find that I no longer want to come out against an injunction, but rather that my intuition of social justice is now that an injunction ought to issue, just as I initially thought the law required. But this is only one of many possible modes of interaction and ultimate equilibration of the law and HIWTCO. Here are some of the other possibilities.

I move the law and the law moves me. The outcome may be a modification of HIWTCO that brings it into accord with a new view of the field, one substantially different from my initial apprehension. Such a compromise might involve conceding that these workers went too far, though the law will not enjoin all lie-ins. Or it might involve not enjoining these workers but conceding that my initial pro lie-in position went much too far, so the workers better not take the next step they appear to be contemplating.

Such a compromise, like restatement of the law to correspond to HIWTCO, or conversion of HIWTCO to correspond to the law, has the peculiarity of *resolving* the initial perceived conflict. But this may not happen. The law may move me, and I may move the law, but the two may end up still in conflict, albeit less in conflict. It's also possible that the normative pull of the field will leave me confused or ambivalent, where I had earlier been quite clear about HIWTCO. Or the reverse might happen: a vague sense of HIWTCO ends up clarified through the imagined dialogue with the ancients. As always, from inside the practice of legal argument the outcome is radically indeterminate.

✧   ✧   ✧

How it sometimes doesn't work

What I have just described might be called the counter-ideal to the scenario in which I manipulate the law-field to correspond to HIWTCO. Here, the law field manipulates HIWTCO, stimulating first ambivalence and then perhaps outright conversion to the other side. But the field is no more necessarily normatively powerful than I am necessarily manipulatively powerful.

To have normative power, the field must present itself as objectively favoring an outcome. Since normative power resides in

the voice of the ancients, which is also just the voice of my ambivalent other half, I must be able to "read" the field in order to
feel its power. The field must present itself as at least somewhat
impacted, rather than as unrationalized, collapsed, contradictory,
or loopified. What I mean by those configurations is just that I
can't integrate the cacophony of ancient voices into a single voice
with a message. The disordered fields may influence me in the
sense that after exposure to them HIWTCO changes in one direction or another. But they are not exercising normative power,
by which I mean the power to persuade me to a view you are trying to persuade me to.

But even supposing I have a sense of how the law comes out
which I can contrast with HIWTCO, it does not follow that the
field will exercise normative power. The message I apprehend as "the
law" is at several removes from a conviction of my own about what
I want to do. It is a message I have to decode, rather than a thought
immediately accessible to me inside my own mind (without making
too much of the mediate/immediate distinction). There will always
be an element of mystery as to whose message it is, whether I have
properly understood it, whether it is "applicable" here at all. Until
I "make it my own" and begin to argue the side of the law against
HIWTCO, the message hovers between the life I can give it and
the status of dead formula.

The message is from the past, from people who put it together in
the past (including my past self, if I was involved). Even if I can understand it and enter into it, it is yesterday's newspaper, queer-look-
ing because so much has happened that it doesn't and couldn't take
into account. The message that is the field was not developed by a
clairvoyant as a message to the future; it is the product of judges
deciding cases and writing opinions to deal with their problems,
though with an eye toward the shape of the field for future cases.
The way we constructed the field dates it and thereby deprives it of

the normative bite it would have if it spoke in the voice of someone
looking over my shoulder as I study the facts of the lie-in.

✧   ✧   ✧

The message was composed by other people, though I may have
played a small part myself. I conceded that just about any message I
can understand will have some normative power, if it is a normative
message. That I can understand it at all means that there was another
person out there thinking about this problem, with that degree of
community with me that mere personhood alone is enough to establish. From that communal identification, however limited it may be,
comes the power to move me just by saying "you ought to do thus
and so." But there are others and there are others.

I will interpret the field as a message from particular others of a
particular historical moment, and, as I particularize, I may find myself less and less convinced. The architects of the law of labor relations
applicable here were turn-of-the-century conservative state court
judges and New Deal reformers. I have mixed feelings about both
groups and about the legal structures of which these by-ways of labor
law form a part. At least, my own evaluation of the message and its
senders seems to have a great effect on how and how strongly I feel it.
Moreover, there are other pulls beside the normative one that I know
are there but whose individual contributions to the force field around
me are indistinguishable, at least as I initially experience them.

✧   ✧   ✧

Influences on the relation between HIWTCO and the law other than the normative power of the field

I have been describing how I ultimately want to come out as
the product of an interaction between my evolving apprehension of
the law field and my intuition of social justice. In my experience,
this interaction is partly a series of events that is happening to me.

It is also partly a series of events that I am making happen through my interpretive construction of the field, which powerfully affects its normative power. But it turns out that my initial intuition of justice under the circumstances is open to influences other than the normative power of the field.

I consult my "gut" against the background of my situation as a judge. In that situation there are definite advantages and disadvantages to a rapprochement between HIWTCO and the law as it now appears to me. I have interests in agreeing with the law and interests in maintaining my disagreement. I worry that these are powerfully modifying what the outcome would have been in their absence—what it would have been had I dealt only with an intuition of justice and a law field capable of exercising normative power.

I also worry about their status: are these influences that should be resisted or that should be treated as legitimately normative in the same way the voice of the ancients is legitimately normative?

The principal influences against merging HIWTCO into whatever I think the law may be—the principal sources of non-normative resistance to the normative power of the field—are the psychological cost of conversion and terror of the disaster of false conversion. On the other side, the principal non-normative influence pushing HIWTCO in the direction of what I see as the law is fear that I won't be able to develop a plausible legal argument for my position, with attendant unpleasant consequences no matter what course of action I undertake.

I am going to discuss these various cost and benefits as influences on HIWTCO—that is, as constitutive of my experienced conviction about the proper outcome. This is odd. It might seem more appropriate to discuss costs and benefits as elements in my decision about what to do, when and if it appears there is an irreconcilable difference between the law and HIWTCO. Indeed, all these costs and benefits of divergence will again become relevant at the point when "I" have to choose a course of conduct. But I want to take them up here as elements constituting HIWTCO because I believe that they impinge first at this unconscious level—eliminating or exacerbating conflict, rather than setting the terms of its resolution.

These costs and benefits also influence my apprehension of the law. It is important, now that we are in the phase of relativizing HIWTCO, not to lose track of the extent to which I constitute the field, both through my interpretation of its configuration and through the work of legal argument. The gestalt process of interpretation and the work of argument go on under the influence of my fear that, if I disagree with the law, I will be forced into an untenable corner of civil disobedience or craven surrender, or undergo false conversion. My choice to see the field as, say, contradictory rather than as impacted in an unfavorable way will be in part a product of my interest in seeing it that way, given my fear of a sharp conflict with HIWTCO.

✧   ✧   ✧

The costs of conversion

I don't want to be converted to the view that I should enjoin the lie-in. My initial opinion that there should be no injunction is in character: as soon as it occurs to me I hold it dear as an emanation of my true self. Like a collection of knick-knacks, my opinions, along with my past, my work, my family, are a store of treasures I don't want to give up.

My social identity, moreover, is bound up with the ritual of agreeing, publicly, with others about issues like this. Other people see me as a person who holds particular kinds of views, and they like me or dislike me partly on that basis (however lamentable such superficiality on their part may be). I'm dependent on their good opinion. If I change my views, some will regard me as a turncoat, as weak-willed or stupid, a fluff-head or an opportunist.

Those who tend to favor management aren't likely to form favorable opinions that will make up for what I lose by conversion, since they won't know whether to trust me. Still worse, perhaps, is my sense that those who hold the view I might convert to—that the injunction should issue—are a bunch I'd hate, as of now, to join. When I think of myself as one of them, I shrink from my imagined turncoat self.

Legal argument, in which I take up and work with the message of the field, and maybe end up espousing it against my current correct and virtuous position, looks like working in a nuclear plant at the risk of radiation sickness. It looks like fooling around with heroin: you think you have it under control, and one morning you wake up already addicted. You've gone from one (good) state to another (bad) state without ever having a moment of choice about it.

I think this fear of being converted without choice, somehow forced from one's own view into another, is deep in almost everyone involved with law. It leads progressive-minded people to ask things like, "Will law school warp my mind?" Or to assert that they think something is legally right but totally morally wrong. Or that law is made-up noise that reinforces things as they are, so it's not worth the trouble to argue within its terms (even though it's manipulable) when the facts cry out for direct moral response.

Even if in contemplation I admit that the conversion might be to a "better view," I still don't want it to happen. Just because it's a better view doesn't mean that moving to it is painless. I don't want to be converted, but I do believe in the possibility of progress in my own views. I believe things now that I used to think were stupid, and I think I'm better off for having been through the process of enlightenment, however painful. So my fear of conversion is qualified by my longing for truth and for change and interesting conflict.

✧   ✧   ✧

I may still be deeply influenced against the normative power of the law-field by the fear of *false conversion*. Maybe what looks like a very compelling legal, moral, utilitarian, political argument against

HIWTCO has a flaw a mile wide. Maybe the company's lawyers even know it does, and maybe I'll be suckered into believing it because I lack constructive as well as critical argumentative ability. (I might be great most of the time but have screwed up here, despite my previous record.) If this happens, I will experience a momentary pleasure of conversion (with attendant mild pains), followed by a subsequent devastating awakening to my own mistake, then humiliation if I change my mind back, and shame if I find myself unable to admit my error and forced to persist in pretending my new wrong position is right.

My sense that I'd better hold on tight to HIWTCO, insulate it against the power of the field, is strengthened by my knowledge that it's not only normative power that's in play here. There is something pure and cutely idealistic about listening to the ancients because one thinks what they have to say may be of value in one's search for the ethically correct result. But suppose that I'm drawn into a false conversion not by earnest openness to enlightenment but by my opportunistic interest in avoiding controversy? I resist the normative power of the field in part because I distrust my own construction of the field.

✧   ✧   ✧

Reasons for converting HIWTCO to correspond to the law (other than the normative power of the field)

It's not that a divergence between HIWTCO (no injunction) and the obvious legal solution ("of course the employer can get an injunction") has to produce trouble for me. Although I am out of line, I may be able to persuade people that I have the better legal case; indeed, the divergence may be the occasion for me to increase my fund of credibility. But if there is a divergence, and I persist in my position rather than letting myself be persuaded that I was wrong and "the law" was right, I have to be ready for the possibility that I will be unable to produce a plausible legal argument for my position. If this happens, I will be in a corner. I may not be able to avoid a painful controversy.

Fear of this controversy will influence how I see both HIWTCO and the field, and influence them in such an intrinsic, automatic way that I won't be able to be "outside" the influence and neutralize it. Sometimes, in spite of the most intense vigilance on my part, fear has eroded my opposition to an outcome until without ever being aware of it I have "gone over to the other side."

✧   ✧   ✧

The devil's compact

I want to discriminate between more and less crass reasons for abandoning HIWTCO. The less crass is fear of finding myself in violation of the devil's compact: that I will either defend my position as plausibly in accord with law, or change it, or withdraw from the case.

I entered the devil's compact when I took my oath of office as a judge. The compact is between me and an imagined public, but it is also a rough way of describing what I think will be the practice of various real people I know, or who can communicate with me through newspapers, letters, popular magazines, law reviews, or bar journals.

Many people believe there is a sharp distinction between action according to law and lawless action. If it appears to them that I have no plausible legal argument for how I want to come out but, nonetheless persist rather than changing my view or withdrawing from the case, they will say I have violated the elementary meaning of the agreement under which I direct the use of state force.

There are people whose good opinion is important to me whose belief in the devil's compact is such that they will condemn me for violating it even if they think the outcome I favor is the just one. They see it as an aspect of the judge's job that she is supposed to bring about outcomes that are unjust when the law is unjust. If you don't like the job, you shouldn't take it. Once you take it, you either do it or refuse to do it (withdraw from the case).

I was aware when I took office that if I were to publicly reject the compact, I probably would not be allowed to become a judge. When I took the job without raising the issues I am about to raise here, I allowed some people to think that I agreed to the terms of the compact. The fact that many liberals and some conservatives understand it in a way that modifies it so much as to make it almost meaningless is irrelevant to my point. People who believe in the compact were necessary, I imagine, for me to become a judge, and it is with them that I entered the compact.

✧   ✧   ✧

On the other hand, I think the popular conception of law is internally contradictory, embracing the notions that (a) "the law is the law," a determinate result-producing technique, and (b) the law is intrinsically an affair of justice, so that it is always "on the side of right," and lacking any theory at all of how conflicts between (a) and (b) are to be resolved. Lay people tend to be surprised when the law turns out to be plain unjust, and surprised also when it turns out to be indeterminate or patently determined by "external" factors such as controversial ethical or political views.

Furthermore, the devil's compact presupposes a view of the relation between the law and HIWTCO that initiates know is false. The manipulability of the field is much greater than the lay public realizes, even if we concede that there is no intelligible way to answer the quantitative question, "How manipulable?" And the point at which the field "sticks," presenting itself as an objective message there's no way to evade, is much more arbitrary than even the legal profession realizes.

This point at which I am supposed to refuse to exercise my power in favor of the workers, is indeed one of perceived objectivity of the field. But I cannot affirm that it is a point at which the law was "just not on their side," because the problem may be that I was not sufficiently skillful, or didn't have enough time, to find their argument. Even if we *are* at a point of objective field adversity (I can't prove such points don't exist), it is not a point that is part of an intelligible pattern.

If the field constrains the judge only in this arbitrary manner, it doesn't make sense to claim that judicial restraint is the workers' quid pro quo for accepting an unjust outcome in any particular case. The devil's compact, if I try to impute it to the litigants rather than to myself as the judge, is vitiated by a mistake as to fundamental terms, a mistake of which I had prior knowledge.

Suppose that I persist in HIWTCO even though it differs from the law as I perceive it after exhausting my resources of legal argument against it. I will then face a choice such that, whatever I do, I will feel terrible. I therefore have a strong motive to somehow reconceive HIWTCO so that it accords with the law and thereby prevent my painful dilemma from ever reaching the level of consciousness.

✧   ✧   ✧

What determines the outcome of the interaction between the field and HIWTCO?

From inside the practice of legal argument, the only possible answer to this question is that I determine the outcome. As I work to manipulate the law field in the direction of HIWTCO, I have a strong feeling that I am acting in the world, remaking it to fit my intentions. If I manage to restate the law so that it plausibly requires my preferred outcome, I will see this as my accomplishment.

As I develop the case against an injunction of the lie-in, I am restating the law about lie-ins. At some point, I may "get the message" of that law and find myself developing it in my own mind as an argument against the position I have been taking, against HIWTCO. Then at some point I may find that "I am changing my mind" and then that "I have changed my mind." In that case, I will feel that it was my own decision to bring HIWTCO into accord with the law.

It is a little hard to figure out what it means to have an "I" inside me who is capable of changing a "my mind" that is both the same as that "I" and different enough so that "I" can determine it rather than just *being* it. But it is my experience that HIWTCO is undetermined right up to the moment when something has happened that moots the question. I can always change my mind about HIWTCO, and I have on occasion found myself changing my mind very late in the game.

❖   ❖   ❖

This way of putting it, though true to occasional experience, overstates my freedom by making it sound as though I were omnipotent. Remember that even in the first moment of confronting the problem I want to come out one way or another in the context of my life-project as a judge and of the law as I already know it. These contexts are givens that have shaped me before I begin to reshape them. I decide already positioned somewhere, having no choice about that somewhere, able to move only by work that takes time.

As soon as I set to work on the particular law-field, I undergo its influence, an influence that is partly normative and partly the product of my fear of finding HIWTCO ultimately in conflict with the law. On the other side are all my good reasons for sticking to my initial conviction, reasons whose influence I can never fully neutralize.

As I work on the field, following a strategy that has its own internal economy and takes time to execute, the field and HIWTCO change and influence one another and change and influence one another some more. If I am lucky, this process appears to have an unforced inner tendency toward convergence, so that eventually the law and HIWTCO are the same, one way or another. But whether and how this convergence occurs is very much a function of aspects of the situation over which I have little control.

First, there is my initial apprehension of the law field, which I just "get" as impacted, contradictory, or whatever. Then there is my strategy, which takes me down a path I can't know in advance. Although I choose it, I don't control the consequences of my choice, since the field has hidden properties, and I have particular biases and only what skill I can muster for the occasion. Then there is the time factor, which means that sooner or later, if convergence does not occur, I will have to stop working on the field, unsure whether its current state is an irremediable aspect of its "true nature" or an artifact of my blundering.

I am now repositioned, so to speak. It's true that I can still change my mind about HIWTCO and that I am free to make one of a number of choices about how to play things, if HIWTCO and the law as I have reconstructed it are in conflict. But it is also true that I will make these choices constrained by where I started and by all my decisions about how to develop the field. What I have done is irreversible in the sense that I can't just "go back" to the way I used to see things. And I've run out of time to *work* the field backward (or forward). I'm stuck where I am and have to decide from here.

What to do in case of conflict between the law and HIWTCO

My answer to this question is unhelpful: it depends on the circumstances.

1. Go along with the law. In spite of my conviction that social justice requires me to deny the injunction, I issue it, along with an opinion denouncing the law and urging reform. I make the very convincing legal argument for an injunction that comes to mind in an impacted field such as this one. A crucial question is how I explain my obedience, that is, my willingness to act as the instrument of injustice.

2. Withdraw from the case. I neither issue the injunction nor deny it. I withdraw, explaining that I think the law is unjust and that my feelings against it make it inappropriate for me to preside and repugnant to me to be involved in administering this regime. A crucial question is how I justify begging off while insisting that someone else do the dirty work, if I intend to stick around for the more attractive assignments.

3. Decide against the injunction on the basis of what the law should be. I deny the injunction, honestly explaining my inability to come up with a plausible legal argument against it. Though I may be reversed on appeal (and quickly at that), I exercise what power I have to further HIWTCO. This may be decisive if the litigants are evenly matched out in the world. I accept what consequences my bureaucratic superiors and my colleagues and peers decide to inflict (highly indeterminate). I appeal to them to accept my outcome as the correct one in this and future cases, thereby changing the law. A crucial question is who authorized me to take the law into my own hands.

4. Decide against the injunction on the basis of an implausible legal argument. Maybe it will look good to others, even though I think it stinks; I can never be sure in advance. Maybe it will turn out in my own hindsight to be a better argument than I thought. But what about the dishonesty of bad faith argument?

5. Decide against the injunction on the basis of fact findings I know to be false. As the trial judge, I decide to pretend to believe an account of the facts of the lie-in that I know to be false, and deny the injunction on that basis. This is obviously an extreme measure.

Afterword

The rule of law

I can imagine hypothetical situations in which each of these courses of action in the face of conflict would be appropriate. I don't think any of them can be either endorsed or excluded a priori. But I am aware that it is often argued that the meaning of the rule of law is obedience to the devil's compact, and that the only permissible course of action for a judge confronting a conflict between the law and how he wants to come out is *always* to follow the law.

Given the practice of judging as I have just presented it, and especially given the apparently arbitrary character of eruptions of perceived objectivity in the course of manipulation, I find this argument unconvincing. But that is for another time. From within the perspective of my imagined judge, the story is over when she reaches the moment of decision. Whether she should *always* follow the law in cases of conflict is a question that we answer as best we can through reflection and argument about our political system, about the actual laws in force within that system, and about particular cases.

Social theory

The judge has to decide what to do from a position. That position depends on the givens of the judge's life-project, on the body of legal materials and the facts of the case as grasped at the beginning of the process, and on the work the judge has done on those materials and facts. In deciding, the judge risks but may also gain credibility, depending on the obviousness gap between the common perception of "the law" and HIWTCO.

On this basis, we might hypothesize that the probability that a judge will move the law so as to achieve any given result is smaller in proportion as the work and the credibility risk involved are greater, and that the total quantity and quality of work available from the judicial labor force limit the total amount of legal movement we can expect in any direction.

For this hypothesis to be useful in studying the role of law in a given social formation, we would have to study both the legal materials and the culture of judges in order to determine, by an essentially imaginative rather than positive procedure, how they are likely to construct given fields, and how much work will appear to them to be involved in different kinds of field manipulations. We would also need to know how often divergences between their initial apprehension of the law and how-they-want to-come-out will motivate them to work hard at manipulation and risk credibility. On the basis of such knowledge, we might speak meaningfully of law as a general constraint on the exercise of state power in the society in question.

Note that without this "internal" information about how judges perceive law fields the notion of law as a constraint on state power is essentially meaningless. We have to know "constrained in what position from moving what distance" before we know anything at all. Note also that this hypothesis is merely "inertial." It says nothing about "inherent tendencies" of the legal materials to develop in particular directions. The total available labor time may be deployed in any way at all, but that it is limited means that movement is constrained.

Whether this description of judging could form the basis of a theory of "inherent tendencies" or directions of development of legal materials is a very difficult question. On the one hand, the judge experiences the normative power of the field as directed toward a particular outcome, and we might develop a social psychology of what this direction will be for a given body of materials. On the other, the field moves only because the judge moves it, and this he does in accord with how-he-wants to come-out, under the constraint of having to work at manipulation and to risk credibility.

A sufficiently complex social psychology might allow us to describe meaningfully the way in which a judiciary with a particular set of political commitments will interact with fields it experiences as having normative power in particular directions. But the notion that the normative power of law fields is directed toward particular patterns of substantive outcomes seems to me tenuous, at least at the moment.

Of course, most social theorists simply assume that "law" is one thing or another and can be treated as a kind of block contributing to a larger edifice. To the extent the experience of law is as I have described it, this approach makes little sense.

Jurisprudence

Imagine you are a professor of jurisprudence, in possession of professional knowledge of the nature of law. Suppose you approach me in my dark cloud of ignorance of whether or not I will be able to overcome the gap between the law and how-I-want-to-come-out. You argue that legal rules, like the rule that the workers can't interfere with the owner's use of the m.o.p. during a strike, *never* determine the outcome of a case. And since the legal rules are the only things that stand in the way of my coming out the way I want to come out, I have no problem. Legal theory indicates that I am home free, or at least that I ought to be home free. If I'm not, it's because I've failed at legal argument, not because of any properties inherent to the field I'm trying to manipulate.

You can expect me, in my role of humble law artificer, to ask you how you can be so sure. You might respond that since Wittgenstein we know that no rule can determine the scope of its own application. It follows more or less directly (unless you insist on a detour through semiotics, structuralism, and deconstruction) that the mere statement, "the workers can't interfere with the owner's use of the m.o.p. during a strike," tells us *nothing* about whether or not they can lie in to block substitute workers from driving the buses out of the garage onto the great American highway. There is a whole world of interpretation, inherently subjective and indeed perhaps even inherently arbitrary (from the standpoint of my humble artificer's idea of reason), that we have to go through to get from the rule to "the facts." And "of course" the facts aren't any more "just there" than the rule.

My experience with legal argument doesn't allow me to meet your jurisprudential position on its own ground. What I can say as a legal arguer is that sometimes I come up against the rule as a felt objectivity, and can't budge it. This doesn't mean that I agree with it or that I think anyone would necessarily condemn me if I disregarded or changed it. All it means is that I say to myself, "Here's the rule that applies to this case;" "we all know that this is the rule;" and "here's how it applies;" and "Everyone is going to apply it that way."

I am perfectly aware that the rule is not a physical object and that deciding how to apply it involves a social, hence in some sense a subjective process. But there is this procedure I've performed many times in my mind, in many different contexts, of applying a rule to a fact situation. I've many times had discussions with others in which we formulated rules together, seemed to agree about their terms, then engaged in a series of applications, and found that once we'd agreed on the formula we came up with the same answer to the question: how does the rule apply *here?*

I believe that it is possible to communicate with another person so that we both have roughly the same rule in mind. I believe that it is possible to communicate with another so we both have roughly the same fact situation in mind. And I believe that when we both come up with the same answer to the question, "How does the rule apply to the facts," it is sometimes meaningful to describe what has happened as "we applied the rule to the facts."

In the situation I most fear as a liberal law-reforming judge, when I have studied the various rules that I think might apply to the lie-in, I conclude that everyone will agree that the employer has a right to an injunction under the rules as we all understand them to be as of now, and that to change this particular rule would be unconstitutional. This conviction might be based on an "identical" case decided by the Supreme Court yesterday, or it might be based on a rather long and abstract chain of reasoning by analogy. But it might happen. And if it happened I would face some pretty tough choices about what to do in the case.

As I said, this declaration of faith in the possibility of communication and in the at least occasional intelligibility of the procedure of rule application doesn't meet your fancy argument on its own ground. I have no idea why this stuff happens. As I see it, your fancy argument is that I can't show an "objective basis" or a rationale or an explanation of rule application that will prove that any particular application was "correct." Indeed, the notion of correctness, at least as we usually use the word in math or science or logic just isn't applicable.

From my position inside the practice of legal argument, I can't say anything one way or another about this fancy argument. I have no way of knowing, from inside the practice, why it is that sometimes the field gives way but sometimes refuses to budge at all. Maybe when it seems unbudgeable it's just because I didn't find the catch that releases the secret panel. Maybe my sense that we communicated the rule to one another and then each "applied" it and that that's where the result "came from" is a false sense, a hopeful or sentimental or, in this lie-in case, a paranoid interpretation of the random fact that we agreed on the outcome, rather than a reflection of a common experience. From inside the practice of argument, I just don't know.

I will be very irritated indeed if you turn around on me now and reveal that you were just using the fancy argument to make me concede the truth of some form of positivism or objectivism about law, or at least legal rules. It was a good trick, but I claim to have evaded it. I have been saying all along that legal argument is the process of creating the field of law through re-statement rather than rule application. Rule application is something that does happen, but I *never* experience it as something that *has* to happen. It is an outcome as contingent and arbitrary from the point of view of jurisprudence as that in which the field is gloriously manipulable.

I dealt here with a case in which my initial apprehension was that the law was clear against the workers, but I was able to undermine the perceived objectivity of the rule (at least in a preliminary way). That was an example among many possible of how an initial apprehension of ruledness can dissolve. Sometimes I approach the field in an agnostic frame of mind, and just can't figure out what the rule is supposed to be; sometimes I can't decide whether the facts are such that the outcome specified by the rule is triggered or not. Sometimes it seems there are several possible answers to the question and I don't have any feeling about which is correct. Sometimes I'm initially quite sure what the rule is and how to apply it but a conversation with another person who has reached a different set of conclusions leaves me feeling neither that I was "right" nor that she was "right," but rather that the rule was in fact hopelessly ambiguous or internally contradictory all along.

If you tell me that there is always a right answer to a legal problem, I will answer with these cases in which my experience was that the law was indeterminate, or that I gave it its determinate shape as a matter of my free ethical or political choice. It is true that when we are unselfconsciously applying rules together, we have an unselfconscious experience of social objectivity. We know what is going to happen next by mentally applying the rule as others will, and then they apply the rule and it comes out the way we thought it would. But this is not in fact objectivity, and it is *always* vulnerable to different kinds of disruption—intentional and accidental—that suddenly disappoint our expectations of consensus and make people question their own sanity and that of others. This vulnerability of the field, its plasticity, its instability, are just as essential to it as we experience it as its sporadic quality of resistance.

The rule may at any given moment appear objective; but at the next moment it may appear manipulable. It is not, *as I apprehend it from within the practice of legal argument,* essentially one thing or the other.

If this is what it is like to ask the nature of law from within the practice of legal argument, then the answer to the question must come from outside that practice. All over the United States and indeed all over the world there are professors of jurisprudence who think they possess professional knowledge of the nature of law. Where are they getting it from? For my own part, I think their answers to questions like those I have been addressing are just made up out of whole cloth. Show me your ground before you pretend to be moving the earth.

1.   Note on sources: I think of this exercise as an extension of the legal realist project, as exemplified in Felix Cohen, The Ethical Basis of Legal Criticism, 41 *Yale L. J.* 201 (1931), Karl N. Llewellyn, *The Common Law Tradition: Deciding Appeals* (1960), and Edward H. Levi, *An Introduction to Legal Reasoning* (1949). The description of legal materials as presenting a field open to manipulation owes much to Wolfgang Kohler, *Gestalt Psychology: An Introduction to New Concepts in Modern Psychology* (New York, 1947), Kurt Lewin, The Conceptual Representation and the Measurement of Psychological Forces, 1 *Contributions to Psychological Theory* 4 (1938), and Jean Piaget, *Play, Dreams, and Imitation in Childhood*, trans. C. Gattegno and F. Hodgson (New York, 1962). My emphasis on work derives from Karl Marx, Economic and Philosophical Manuscripts of 1844-1845, *in Early Works*, trans. Benton (New York, 1975). The overall conception and philosophical premises derive loosely from Jean-Paul Sartre, *Being and Nothingness.* trans. Hazel Barnes (New York, 1956) and Jean-Paul Sartre, *Critique of Dialectical Reason*, trans. Alan Sheridan-Smith (London, 1976).

A SEMIOTICS OF LEGAL ARGUMENT

Table of Contents

I.   Introduction

II.   Dictionary Entries

III. Argument by Maxim and Counter-maxim
    A. Typology of Argument-Bites in Pairs
        1. Substantive Arguments
            (a) Moral Arguments
            (b) Rights Arguments
            (c) Social Welfare Arguments
            (d) Expectations Arguments
        2. Systemic Arguments
            (a) Administrability Arguments
            (b) Institutional Competence Arguments
    B. Remarks on Argument by Counter-Bite

IV.   Operations in Legal Argument
    A. Typology of Operations
        1. Denial of a (Factual or Normative) Premise
        2. Symmetrical Opposition
        3. Counter-Theory
        4. Mediation
        5. Refocusing on Opponent's Conduct (Proposing an Exception)
        6. Flipping
        7. Level-Shifting
    B. Concluding Remark on Operations

V.   Support Systems and Clusters
    A. Support Systems
    B. Clustering
        1. Formalities Cluster
        2. Compulsory Terms Cluster

C. Concluding Remark on the Interdependence of the
    Meanings of Argument-Bites

VI. Nesting

VII. Conclusion

Appendix I: Methodological Origins of this Semiotics of
             Legal Argument
    A. Argument-Bites
    B. Operations
    C. Nesting

Appendix II: Responses to Four European Objections
    A. The Arguments Identified are Not Present as
        Stereotyped Bites in European Legal
        Argumentative Practice
    B. The Bites Analysis is Just Another Example of the
        Theory that Law is Rhetoric
    C. No Rule Can Determine the Scope of its Own
        Application
    D. The Analysis of Policy Argument is Irrelevant
        for Europe Because European Law is Formal,
        Certain and Legislative by Contrast with American
        Law

I. Introduction

My impression is that when people interested in legality appropriate the theory or philosophy of language, they tend to focus on the rule form and the "facts" in the world to which the rules are applied. For example, what does language theory tell us about the meaning of a statement such as "you must be 35 years old to be eligible for election to the Presidency?" In this paper, I pursue a different kind of borrowing, focusing on what language theory might offer the as yet rudimentary theory of legal argument.

By legal argument, I mean argument in favor of or against a particular resolution of a gap, conflict, or ambiguity in the system of legal rules. In this form of argument, it is the practice to deploy stereotyped "argument-bites," such as, "my rule is good because it is highly administrable." Argument-bites come in opposed pairs, so that the above phrase is likely to be met with, "but your rule's administrability comes from such rigidity that it will do serious injustice in many particular cases."

Starting with the argument-bite as a basic unit, I propose a set of inquiries into legal argument, using language theory as a source of analogies. First, there is the lexicographical or "mapping" enterprise of trying to identify the most common bites. Second, there is an inquiry into the generation of pairs and their clustering into dialectical sequences, rituals of parry and thrust. The response above might be answered, "there will be few serious injustices in particular cases because my rule is knowable in advance (unlike your vague standard) and parties will adjust their conduct accordingly." Third, there is the second-order mapping task of identifying "clusters" of arguments (some candidates: formalities as a precondition for legally effective expressions of intent, compulsory contract terms, existence and delimitation of legally protected interests, liability for unintended injury).

The fourth inquiry is into the consequences of the argument-bite idea for the phenomenology of legal argument. If arguments come in stereotypical bites, then it is at least plausible (1) that they get their meaning from one another, in the sense that words do, (2) that to be intelligible to a legal audience one must stretch one's thought on their Procrustean bed, so that there is always a gap or discontinuity between the subject and his or her argument, something at once constrained and strategic about the choice of distortions, and (3) that the course of the legal argument will be at least somewhat independent of the particular topic, that is the particular gap, conflict or ambiguity in the rule system to which it is apparently quite specifically addressed, so that argument is the play of argument-bites (as well as an evocation of the possibilities of a real situation of choice).

It is an interesting question whether legal argument is possible in its highly self-serious contemporary mode only because the participants are at least somewhat naive about its simultaneously structured and indeterminate (floating) character. The rest of this paper is mainly concerned with the first two tasks: that of developing a lexicon and that of attempting to identify some of the operations or transformations of argument-bites that legal arguers use to generate a meaningful exchange.

II. Dictionary Entries

The following is a list of argument-bites in random order. It is of course not exhaustive, but rather fragmentary. The two principles of selection will become clear below.

legal protection of the fruits of labor gives an incentive to production

the proposed solution will be easy to administer

no liability without fault

only the legislature can obtain the information necessary to make this decision rationally

the defendant should have looked out for the plaintiff's interests (altruistic duty) the law, not community expectations, should determine the outcome

the proposed solution lacks equitable flexibility

people have a right to freedom of (this kind of) action

the defendant's immunity will discourage the plaintiff's desirable activity

judges make decisions every day with no more information than they have here

pacta sunt servanda (promises should be kept, period)

the defendant's liability will discourage the plaintiff from looking out for himself (i.e., from taking precautions)

the proposed rule defeats the defendant's expectation of freedom of action

as between two innocents he who caused the damage should pay

the plaintiff should have looked out for his own interests (been self-reliant)

the role of the judge is to apply the law, not make it

legal protection inhibits competition in markets for goods and ideas

the proposed rule corresponds to community expectations

no such right has ever been recognized at common law, so the judge has no power to intervene

there is prima facie liability for intentional harm in the absence of an excuse

the proposed rule protects the plaintiff's reliance

the common law evolves to meet new social conditions

people have a right to be secure from (this kind of) injury

liability will discourage the defendant's desirable activity

liability will encourage the defendant to take precautions

rebus sic stantibus (only as long as circumstances remain the same)

III. Argument by Maxim and Counter-maxim

I selected this particular randomly ordered list because I can use its members to illustrate a basic structure of legal argument, namely the pairing of arguments as maxim and counter-maxim. Another way to put this is to say that a competent legal arguer can, in many (most? all?) cases, generate for a given argument-bite at least one counter argument-bite that has an equal status as valid utterance within the discourse. While responding to an argument-bite with one of its stereotypical counter-bites may be wholly unpersuasive to the audience, it is never incorrect, at least not in the sense in which it would be incorrect to answer an argument-bite with an attack on the speaker's character or with a description of the weather.

This selection of argument-bites also allows me to propose a tentative typology, which I will use to order my pairs, but not further explain or justify here. The categories are substantive argument-bites, used to characterize party behavior in relation to the proposed rule, and systemic bites, used to characterize the rule in terms of the institutional values of the legal system. I subcategorize substantive arguments in terms of their sources in general political/ethical discourse as based on morality, rights, social welfare or community expectations. Among systemic bites, I distinguish those that have to do with administrability from those that refer to conflicting theories of the role of courts vis-à-vis legislatures (institutional competence arguments).

I have omitted the whole category of arguments about the correct interpretation of authorities (e.g., arguments to the effect that a precedent does or does not "govern," that a statute does or does not "cover" the case). But it is worth noting that the "policy" arguments below are often deployed to support a particular interpretation of a case or statute, or to resolve a conflict of authority, as well as to deal with cases understood to be "of first impression."

A. A Typology of Argument-Bites in Pairs

1. Substantive Arguments

   (a) Moral Arguments

   the defendant should have looked out for the plaintiff's interests (altruistic duty)
   vs.
   the plaintiff should have looked out for his own interests (been self-reliant)

   as between two innocents he who caused the damage should pay
   vs.
   no liability without fault

   pacta sunt servanda (promises should be kept, period)
   vs.
   rebus sic stantibus (only as long as circumstances remain the same)

   (b) Rights Arguments

   people have a right to be secure from (this kind of) injury
   vs.
   people have a right to freedom of (this kind of) action

   (c) Social Welfare Arguments

   the defendant's immunity will discourage the plaintiff's desirable activity
   vs.
   liability will discourage the defendant's desirable activity

   liability will encourage the defendant to take precautions
   vs.

the defendant's liability will discourage the plaintiff from looking out for himself (i.e., from taking precautions)

legal protection of the fruits of labor gives an incentive to production
vs.
legal protection inhibits competition in markets for goods and ideas

(d) Expectations Arguments

the proposed rule corresponds to community expectations
vs.
the law, not community expectations, should determine the outcome

the proposed rule protects the plaintiff's reliance
vs.
the proposed rule defeats the defendant's expectation of freedom of action

2. Systemic Arguments

(a) Administrability Arguments

the proposed solution will be easy to administer
vs.
the proposed solution lacks equitable flexibility

(b) Institutional Competence Arguments

no such right has ever been recognized at common law, so the judge has no power to intervene
vs.
there is prima facie liability for intentional harm absent an excuse

the role of the judge is to apply the law, not make it
vs.
the common law evolves to meet new social conditions

only the legislature can obtain the information necessary
to make this decision rationally
vs.
judges make decisions every day with no more information
than they have here.

B. Remarks on Argument by Counter-Bite

The phenomenon of the counter-maxim is complex. The following remarks are no more than suggestive. First, argument-bites are conventional. What makes a particular sentence an argument-bite is nothing more nor less than that people use it over and over again (or use a phrase that is its equivalent in their understanding) with a sense that they are making a move, or placing a counter in the game of argument.

Second, each argument-bite is associated in the minds of arguers not with one but with a variety of counter-bites. The list above illustrates only a few of the modes of opposition of bites. I will shortly attempt a typology of oppositional moves, or operations.

Third, an extended argument for a particular resolution of a gap, conflict or ambiguity in the rule system will be only relatively structured. In other words, only a part of the material will be recognizable as the play of bites. Arguments occur in particular contexts, and these contexts give them content that is arbitrary from the point of view of structural analysis. It is rarely productive to take the structural point of view to the extreme of reducing everything in the argument to the mechanical reproduction of moves or operations.

Fourth, it is nonetheless true that every legal argument within a legal culture is by definition relatively structured. Indeed, this is what we mean when we situate the argument in our legal culture, rather than in lay discourse or philosophical discourse or (to pick an example at random) French legal culture.

IV. Operations in Legal Argument

By an operation I mean a "transformation" of an argument-bite by "doing something" to it that gives it a very different meaning, but one that is nonetheless connected to the starting bite. The prototype of an operation, as I am using the term here, is the simple procedure of adding "not" to a phrase, so as to indicate that it is untrue rather than true, as in "I am not French." This phrase is obviously closely related to "I am French," although it has an altogether different meaning[!?!].

The power of structuralist methodology is that it shows that what at first appears to be an infinitely various, essentially contextual mass of utterances (parole) is in fact less internally various and less contextual than that appearance. It does this by "reducing" many of the particular elements of the discourse to the status of operational derivatives of other elements.

When I say, "I am French," and you respond, "No, you are not French," there is less going on, less complexity to deal with, than if you responded, "I don't understand your agenda." The reason being that "you are not French" adds a new meaning to the conversation through a simple, familiar transformation of, an operation on, "I am French," rather than by adding what appears, at least at first, an altogether new thought.

A. A Typology of Operations

1. Denial of a (Factual or Normative) Premise

Argument by denial means accepting the relevance of your opponent's argument but denying one of its factual or normative premises. For example:

(morality)
no liability without fault
vs.
I agree that there should be no liability without fault, but you were at fault here, so you are liable.

(morality)
pacta sunt servanda (promises should be kept, period)
vs.
there was no promise

(morality)
pacta sunt servanda (promises should be kept, period)
vs.
True, but I kept my promise

(rights)
plaintiff has a right to security from (this kind of) injury
vs.
this kind of right exists, but defendant did not injure plaintiff

(rights)
plaintiff has a right to security from (this kind of) injury
vs.
no such right exists

(utility)
liability will discourage defendant's desirable activity
vs.
liability will not in fact discourage the activity

(utility)
liability will discourage defendant's desirable activity
vs.
defendant's activity is undesirable

(administrability)
the proposed solution will be easy to administer
vs.
the proposed rule is not in fact administrable

Denial of a factual premise will typically lead to a reframing of the facts presented by the other side so as to support the attack. Classic reframing techniques exploit the ambiguities of crucial concepts like fault, causation and free will to reverse an opponent's presentation.

2. Symmetrical Opposition

The most striking form of oppositional pairing is between two maxims appealing respectively to the plaintiff's and the defendant's points of view as it will always be possible to argue them within a particular cluster. Some examples:

(morality)
the defendant should have looked out for the plaintiff's interests (altruistic duty)
vs.
the plaintiff should have looked out for his own interests (been self-reliant)

(rights)
plaintiff has a right to be secure from (this kind of) injury
vs.
defendant has a right to freedom of (this kind of) action

(utility)
liability will discourage defendant's desirable activity
vs.
immunity will discourage plaintiff's desirable activity

(utility)
legal protection of the fruits of labor gives an incentive to production
vs.
legal protection inhibits competition in markets for goods and ideas

(expectations)
the proposed rule protects the plaintiff's reliance
vs.
the proposed rule defeats the defendant's expectation of freedom of action

(administrability)
the proposed solution will be easy to administer
vs.
the proposed solution lacks equitable flexibility

This operation might be called "Hohfeldian opposition" rather than "symmetrical opposition," since it was Hohfeld who first identified the ambiguity in our common legal usage of the word "right" that often masks it when we are speaking in the rights mode. He pointed out that a right understood as a privilege to act without liability was the opposite of a right understood as entitlement to protection from injury, though they were continually referred to using the same word. This once recognized, it is apparent that for every argument in the form, "I have a right (privilege) to do this," there is available, in principle, the symmetrically opposed argument, "I have a right (entitlement) not to be injured in this way." Both arguments are, once both are on the table, patently partial or incomplete, just because each ignores its symmetrical pair.

It seems reasonable to describe the relationship as operational because once one has learned the "trick" of appealing to the defendant's right to freedom of action every time the plaintiff appeals to her right to be secure from this kind of injury, one no longer sees the two arguments as independent.

Likewise with the defendant's protest that liability will chill his desirable activity, and the plaintiff's symmetrical claim that unless protected he will cut back on his highly beneficial pursuits. The appearance of X in close proximity to Y no longer seems a function of the irreducible particularity of context, but rather of the structure of legal argument itself.

Again, this is not to say that the arguments will always be equally convincing. Quite the contrary. Nor that as a matter of fact the appearance of X on the plaintiff's lips will automatically elicit Y on the lips of the defendant. Y may not occur to the defendant. Or it may seem tactically unwise to invoke a right to freedom of action (suppose the issue is civil liability, and the defendant's conduct is indisputably criminal). Yet when Y does occur in response to X, we experience, if we recognize the operation, the relative coherence or intelligibility, as opposed to the relative arbitrariness of legal discourse.

3.   Counter-Theory

By a counter-theory, I mean a response which simply rejects the normative idea in the principal argument-bite. There is no quick shift from one point of view to another, as in symmetrical opposition, but direct confrontation.

(morality)
no liability without fault
vs.
innocent victims should be compensated

(morality)

pacta sunt servanda (promises should be kept, period)
vs.
rebus sic stantibus (only as long as circumstances remain the same)

(expectations)
the proposed rule corresponds to community practice
vs.
the law, not community practice, should determine the outcome

(institutional competence)
no such right has ever been recognized at common law, so the judge has no power to intervene
vs.
there is liability for intentional injury in the absence of an excuse

(institutional competence)
the role of the courts is to apply law, not make it
vs.
the common law evolves to meet new social conditions

4. Mediation

Mediation differs both from symmetrical (or Hohfeldian) opposition and from counter-theory because it acknowledges a conflict of claims and proposes a way to resolve it on the arguer's side. The mediator argues for a principle or a balancing test that will settle the matter, either in general or in this particular case. For example, the counter-theory to "no liability without fault" might be "innocent victims should be compensated." "As between two innocents...," on the other hand, acknowledges a claim on both sides, but proposes a principle of liability based on causation to resolve the conflict.

(principle)
no liability without fault
vs.

as between two innocents he who caused the damage
should pay

(balancing)
innocent victims should be compensated
vs.

as between two innocents, it is cheapest to let the losses lie
where they fall

(balancing)
rebus sic stantibus (only as long as circumstances remain
the same)
vs.

the utility of promise keeping will be undermined if people
see their obligations as merely contextual

(principle)
plaintiff has a right to security from (this kind of) injury
vs.

plaintiff's ordinary right must yield to defendant's fundamental right

(balancing)
plaintiff has a right to security from (this kind of) injury
vs.

defendant's right outweighs plaintiff's right

(balancing)
liability will discourage defendant's desirable activity
vs.

plaintiff's activity is more desirable than defendant's

(balancing)
your proposed solution lacks equitable flexibility

vs.

on balance, the gain in certainty outweighs the lack of flexibility in this case

Mediation requires the arguer to acknowledge the conflict between a pair of superficially powerful arguments that we produced above either by symmetrical opposition or by theory and counter-theory. It is therefore an operation performed on a pair, rather than on a single argument-bite. This should serve to emphasize the point that there is no natural or pre-given unit of analysis in the semiotics of legal argument. Sometimes the appropriate unit seems quite clearly to be the bite, sometimes it seems equally clearly to be a pair of bites, a cluster, or, as we will see, the bite with its support system.

5. Refocusing on Opponent's Conduct (Proposing an Exception)

Refocusing on your opponent's conduct means particularizing within the general context of your opponent's argument. You concede the premise, but point out that she has behaved in a way that makes the valid premise inapplicable in this case. Refocusing differs from denying that the facts support the argument, or denying the normative premise, because it proposes an exception rather than challenging the argument as a whole.

Because there is an almost infinite number of ways in which we can imagine refocusing, it is arguable that we are slipping here over the line between an operation and the multiplicity of arbitrary, contextual, opportunistic, strategic behavior. Yet there is a patterned quality to the responses below. They are quite abstract, and it is easy to apply them in dozens and dozens of contexts without submerging the abstraction in particularity. Refocusing seems at least to merit tentative status as an operation.

(morality)
no liability without fault
vs.
this injury was an anticipated cost of doing business (Pinto)

(morality)
innocent victims should be compensated
vs.
plaintiff could have gotten out of the way (LeRoy Fibre)

(rights)
plaintiff has a right to security from (this kind of) injury
vs.
plaintiff has forfeited his rights by his conduct in this case

(rights)
defendant has a right to freedom of (this kind of) action
vs.
defendant has forfeited his right by his conduct in this case

(utility)
the defendant's immunity will discourage plaintiff's desirable activity
vs.
but if there is liability, plaintiffs will behave strategically (blackmail defendants)
(utility)
liability will discourage defendant's desirable activity
vs.
but if there is immunity, defendants will behave strategically (blackmail plaintiffs)

(administrability)
the proposed solution lacks equitable flexibility
vs.

because the parties can adjust their behaviour to the rule, its lack of equitable flexibility is not important

(administrability)
the proposed solution will be easy to administer
vs.
the inability of some parties to master the formality will accentuate inequality of bargaining power

There is an interesting and important set of stereotypical responses to refocusing, such as that "the exception would swallow the rule," and "the distinction is illusory" ("collapsing the distinction"). Not to mention "loopification." But for another time.

6. Flipping

Flipping is appropriating the central idea of your opponent's argument-bite and claiming that it leads to just the opposite result from the one she proposes:
reverse fault: when a person who innocently injures another innocent refuses to compensate, he is at fault

reverse competition: only the establishment of legal rights to economic advantage will prevent cut-throat competition from leading to monopoly
reverse community expectations: following community expectations would be undemocratic because those expectations have been significantly formed by the prior course of judicial decision

reverse unequal bargaining power: interfering with freedom of contract will lead to pass-through of the cost and impoverish the people you are trying to help

reverse paternalism: to insist in the face of people's actual failings that they be self- reliant is to impose your values on them

reverse administrability: the pursuit of rules in this area has spawned such complexity that a general equitable standard would increase rather than decrease certainty

reverse institutional competence: leaving the decision to the legislature is a form of lawmaking because it establishes the defendant's legal right to injure the plaintiff

7. Level-shifting

It is permissible to answer an argument-bite for the plaintiff with a pro-defendant argument-bite from another pair. Indeed, this is one of the most common ways to argue. I say your rule lacks administrability. You respond that your rule tailors liability to fault. And so on. Level-shifting is a highly "permissive" operation, meaning that there are lots of maxims to choose from when changing the subject. But there is an important restriction. For the shift to make sense, it must be to an argument-bite associated with the particular legal issue at hand. To use a phrase from the next section, it must be to another bite within the cluster.

B. Concluding Remark on Operations

It is easy to fall into the error of believing that what I have been calling operations are a true "logic of legal discourse." We may be able to transform "plaintiff has a right to security from (this kind of) injury" into, "defendant has a right to freedom of (this kind of) action," by the operation of "symmetrical opposition." But it most certainly does not follow (a) that any other maxim can be so transformed, or (b) that any maxim that can be will, in fact, be so transformed by lawyers and judges in practice. Sometimes yes, and sometimes no, depending on ... "the circumstances." I have little confidence that we will be able to establish the actual "scope" of operations in legal argument other than by trial and error.

I constructed my typology in a relatively empirical or pragmatic fashion, by first listing familiar arguments, then inventing a typology, then playing with items and abstractions until time ran out. There was a temptation, once I had defined a set of operations, to invent arguments that are not part of the vocabulary in use, but "ought to be." For example, symmetrical opposition seems a particularly important operation, and it would be satisfying if one could carry it out on every item in the dictionary. As I set out to list examples, I was often in doubt, and found myself trying hard to "come up with" an argument-bite that would show the generality of the operation. For example, is the following pair a "genuine" instance of symmetrical opposition?

> (institutional competence)
> a decision for the plaintiff would be law making, not law application
> vs.
> a decision for the defendant would be law making, not law application

I am not sure. The answer would seem to require a more precise definition of "symmetrical opposition" than I gave above. A more precise definition might well throw into question some of the examples of the operation that at first seemed paradigmatic, and also lead to the generation of new examples. And so on.

The appeal of this activity, of working toward an exhaustive mechanics of transformation, is that it gives the illusion of mastery of a whole discourse. But, as I said before, every actual instance of an extended argument in favor of a particular resolution of a gap, conflict, or ambiguity in a rule system contains large quantities of contextual matter. The contextual matter influences the formulation of the argument-bites that are its grid.

The problem is deeper yet. The distinction between a bite and a merely contextual argument is so blurry, and so much in motion through time, that there is no hope of a definitive dictionary or of a definitive typology of operations (any more than there is with a living language). For example, the distinction between social welfare arguments about activity levels and about precautions was clearly formulated for the first time well after I began to work on this project.

Given the intractability of the discursive mass from which one must mine argument-bites, and the ease with which one can construct them once one has devised some operations, constructed bites threaten to force out their rougher but authentic counterparts. Furthermore, as I developed my typologies, I found myself repeatedly rewriting the one sentence bites in the dictionary, so that they would "fit" better.

Legal semiotic discourse seems (at every moment, and why not?) to replace its object of study with a pseudo-object more amenable to its internal requirements. Why not: the more legal argument and the less semiotic invention we include in the object of study, the more interesting the analysis will be, by which I mean the more political it will be—the more capable of disquieting power.

[And then there is the possibility that the academic study of operations might influence those very operations...]

V. Support Systems and Clusters

In this section, I extend the notion that argument-bites get their meaning, and legal argument gets its intelligibility, from the system of connections between bites.

A. Support Systems

An argument can be more or less developed. At one extreme, it may be one sentence long: "no liability without fault." At another, that one sentence is supported by pages of material. Some of this material will consist of reasons why we should accept the one sentence argument. These reasons may themselves be conventional, to the point that they are best understood as argument-bites, and as constituting a "support system" for the "lead" bite. Since the system of supporting bites is implicitly present in the mind of the arguer when she deploys the lead bite, it should be understood as one of the sources of that bite's meaning, just as the opposing bites, which everyone knows we can generate through operations, are part of that bite's meaning.

I suggested above that we categorize arguments in four substantive modes (morality, rights, utility, and expectations), and two systemic modes (administrability and institutional competence). We often use substantive modes as "ultimates," or arguments that do not need further justification. By contrast, it is more common within legal discourse to see institutional competence and administrability arguments as in need of support from the substantive arguments.

But this is only a matter of convention. In our legal culture, people think of morality, rights, etc., as providing explanations for action that are satisfactory in themselves, but they also, from time to time, choose to "go behind" them. The distinction between substantive and systemic modes is one of degree only. In fact, bites in each mode can support bites in each of the other modes, producing a complex system.

We support institutional competence arguments with sub-arguments in each of the substantive modes. For example:

> judges should be restricted to law application *because* it is inefficient for them to engage in law making
>
> vs.

judges should evolve the common law *because* this will be better for the general welfare than always waiting for the legislature

private actors have a *right* to be free of liability except where there is precedent
vs.
the *community expects* people who injure others without an established privilege to be held liable

it would be *unfair* to the parties for the judge to resolve their case without the kind of information that only the legislature can obtain
vs.
it is *immoral* for the judges to decline jurisdiction on the grounds that someone else might have been able to decide more competently.

The above arguments are reversible ("it is immoral for the judge to meddle with the parties without the kind of information only the legislature can obtain," etc.).

We also support institutional competence arguments with administrability arguments: "judges should apply, not make the law," with, "otherwise there will be hopeless uncertainty." We support administrability arguments with sub-arguments in the four substantive modes ("the certainty of rules—as opposed to the uncertainty of standards—benefits everyone in the society by eliminating unnecessary disputes"), and also with institutional competence arguments ("only a regime of rules, and not a regime of standards, is consistent with the judicial role of law application, as opposed to law making"). In other words, the two types of systemic argument are mutually supporting.

The appeal to expectations can be used in an ultimate way: "the proposed rule is bad because it would violate the expectations of the parties, period." But expectations arguments are often supported in the other three modes: "people have a right to have courts follow their expectations," "it is socially beneficial for courts to follow expectations," "it would be immoral for courts to frustrate expectations." Moreover, we can toss in systemic reasons for following expectations: "following expectations will give law certainty, whereas courts following their own views would be hopelessly uncertain," "the non-democratic nature of courts means they have to follow expectations or be guilty of usurpation." And so on through the other substantive modes.

The ability to generate the support system for an argument-bite, picking and choosing among its elements to fit the context, is as important to the arguer as the ability to "counter-punch" an opponent's bites. Our ability to understand and assess the value of an argumentative sequence is heavily dependent on our imaginative ability to place each bite in its implicit support system, and understand the response to the bite as also a response to that system.

B. Clustering

Although this is not the place for a full discussion, at least a few preliminary thoughts on clustering seem necessary in order to fill out the ways in which argument-bites acquire meaning. A cluster is a set of arguments that are customarily invoked together, when the arguer identifies his raw facts as susceptible of posing a particular kind of legal issue. Argument-bites acquire meaning not only through their oppositional relationship to bites we generate through operations, and not only from their relationship to bites they support and are supported by, but also from the other members of the cluster.

From the great mass of the facts of the case, the lawyer selects those that he or she thinks can be cast as "relevant" to one of the preexisting rule formulae that together compose the corpus juris. Then the lawyer works to recast both facts and formula so that the desired outcome will appear compelled by mere rule application. The argumentative apparatus we have been discussing is, remember, deployed in order to resolve a gap, conflict or ambiguity in the rule system.

The problem is situated for the participants according to which rule or rules need interpretation. The rule, in turn, is situated in one of the conventional or intuitive arrangements of the *corpus juris*. But it is also situated on a map of "types of legal issues" that occur over and over again in different parts of the *corpus juris*. Some examples of these recurring problems are:

(1) Should judges grant any kind of legal protection to the interest asserted by plaintiff? If so, what degree of protection?

(2) Should judges impose liability for this type of unintended, non-negligent injury?

(3) Should judges require a formality before recognizing an expression of (this particular kind of) intent as legally binding? How should they deal with failure to comply?

(4) Should judges impose a non-disclaimable duty on anyone who enters a contract of this particular kind?

To my mind, one of the most urgent tasks of legal semiotics is to identify other clusters of this kind. A disproportionate number of the bites discussed above come from the particular "cluster" that arguers deploy in debates about the definition and delimitation (through defenses) of legally protected interests. There is a distinct intentional torts bias to the whole discussion. Nonetheless, we could begin to break the bites out into clusters as follows:

1. Formalities Cluster

    (denial)
    defendant induced plaintiff's pre-formality or extra-formality reliance, so should compensate plaintiff's loss
    vs.
    defendant did not induce, plaintiff did not rely, plaintiff was not injured

    (symmetrical opposition)

Defendant induced plaintiff's pre-formality or extra-formality reliance, so should compensate plaintiff's loss
vs.
protecting plaintiff's reliance would defeat defendant's expectation of freedom of action up to the moment of formality

(focusing on opponent's conduct)
defendant induced plaintiff's pre-formality or extra-formality reliance, so should compensate plaintiff s loss
vs.
plaintiff's reliance was the product of gullibility and wishful thinking
vs.
defendant was manipulating the formality with full knowledge of the plaintiff's ignorance and naïveté

(symmetrical opposition)
the proposed formality will be easy to administer
vs.
the proposed formality lacks equitable flexibility

(reverse administrability)
the pursuit of rules in the area of formalities has spawned such complexity that a general equitable standard would increase rather than decrease certainty

(refocusing on opponent's conduct)
the proposed formality lacks equitable flexibility
vs.
because the parties can adjust their behaviour to the formality if they want to, it is paternalistic to disregard it after the fact

(reverse paternalism)
to insist in the face of people's actual failings that they self

reliantly adjust their behaviour to the formality is to impose your values on them

(mediation)
the proposed formality will be easy to administer
vs.
the inability of weak parties to master the proposed formality will unacceptably accentuate inequality of bargaining power

(reverse unequal bargaining power)
undermining the formality will lead to pass-through of the cost and impoverish the people you are trying to help.

2. Compulsory Terms Cluster

(counter-theory)
the defendant should not be bound because his choice was unwise
vs.
second guessing the defendant's choice is paternalistic unless he is an infant or insane

(counter-theory)
the defendant should not be bound because the plaintiff had superior bargaining power
vs.
the law has no concern with unequal bargaining power

(flipping)
courts increase social welfare by refusing to enforce contracts based on unequal bargaining power
vs.
interfering with freedom of contract will lead to pass-through of the cost and impoverish the people you are trying to help

(counter-theory)
it's not the role of the courts to make contracts for the parties
vs.
since the equity of redemption, courts have always inter-
vened against over-reaching

And so on.

I argued that the distinction between counter-argument by operation and mere contextual or opportunistic counter-argument is
blurred. Likewise for support systems and clusters. The formalities
cluster blurs into the compulsory terms cluster. In a given context, it
will be hard to distinguish between formulaic argument-bites from a
cluster and arguments more "authentically" emerging from the facts.
A given argument-bite ("no liability without fault") may appear in
many clusters, along with some but not all of its counter-bites.

It may well be impossible to establish an exhaustive list of operations, or to correctly delimit the clusters extant at a given moment in
the history of legal argument. A given argument-bite's counter-maxims, support system and cluster are three indefinite series of associated items. The point is that we listen to the bite, when an opponent
deploys it in a particular doctrinal context, with the other members
of the cluster already in mind. What we hear depends on those un-
spoken bites, just as it depends on each bite's support system and
counter-maxims.

The discussion of "nesting," below, is situated in the cluster that
arguers invoke when they have identified the legal issue as involving
the definition, through specifying defenses, of the contours of a legally protected interest.

C. Concluding Remark on the Interdependence of the Mean-
ings of Argument-Bites

The claim that words "get their meanings" not from the things
or ideas they signify but from their relationships with other words

is often presented in a way that is, to put it mildly, mystifying. I want here to make an analogous claim about argument-bites, but one that seems to me relatively straightforward.

When a practiced legal arguer puts forward a proposition such as "there should be no liability without fault," he or she does so with a professionally heightened sense of those words as "rhetoric." The legal arguer is more aware than the lay arguer, either consciously or close to consciously, that there are counter-arguments derivable by operation, that "no liability without fault" can be supported by sub-arguments based on rights, social welfare, administrability, and so forth, and that this argument is associated with the other arguments in a doctrinal cluster.

To say that the "meaning" of "no liability without fault" depends on its existence in relationship to "as between two innocents, he who caused the damage should pay," is to say that if we imagine eliminating the latter phrase from the vocabulary of argument-bites, then "no liability without fault" would *ipso facto* become a different, and likely a more powerful or valuable argument than it is when it is counterable by "as between two innocents..." Of course, there would still be other counters, such as "but you were at fault." And the situation might be one in which "no liability without fault" seemed a weak or obtuse moral position, even though no stereotyped, familiar "as between two innocents..." counter-bite was available.

It is even possible that working ad hoc, or opportunistically, the other side might develop the very words "as between two innocents ..." as their considered response to the deployment of "no liability without fault" in a particular case. But then "as between two innocents..." would be a somewhat surprising, complex, hard to evaluate, hand-crafted utterance, without the resonance that comes from repetition in thousands of other cases. It might carry the day, but if it did so, it would be as an example of the power of invention tailored to context.

It may at first seem hard to reconcile this thought-experiment, in which we imaginatively eliminate a bite from the lexicon, with the idea that we "generate" "as between two innocents..." from "no liability without fault" by the "operation" of "mediation." If this is the case, how could "as between two innocents..." not be part of the vocabulary of bites?

The answer lies in the fundamental proposition that the possibility of generating a bite by counter-theory does not guarantee that such a bite has in fact been generated, or indeed that such a counter-bite will ever be part of the vocabulary. The system of bites, counter-bites, support systems and clusters that exists at a given moment is a product of the actual history of a particular legal discourse, at the same time that it is the product of the logic of operations. An existing system is always incomplete, looked at from the point of view of possible operations, and always changing as new bites enter the lexicon and others change their form or fall out of use altogether.

Each change of this kind alters the possibilities of legal discourse, because it changes what is available to the arguer as stereotyped argument to be deployed across the range of fact situations as they arise. But each change also changes the meaning and effectiveness of the other bites in the system, because it changes arguers' conscious or unconscious expectations about what will be said in response to those bites. To take a recent example, the phrase "defendant should be liable because she is the cheapest cost avoider" is a new argument-bite. Its presence in the repertoire of numerous legal arguers has changed the meaning of (lessened the value of) "no liability without fault" and also of "as between two innocents..." because neither of them seems at all responsive to it, though both belong to the same cluster of arguments about liability for unintentional injury.

The emergence of "she is the cheapest cost avoider" has also changed the two traditional bites in a more subtle way. "No liability without fault" has as part of its support system a "social welfare argument" to the effect that "there is no social interest in shifting the costs of blameless activity." On the other side, "as between two innocents..." is supported by "activities should be made to internalize their true social costs." It is still unclear to what extent, if any, these support-bites retain coherence after the emergence of "she is the cheapest cost avoider." Even if it turns out that the support bites are still sensible, the primary bites will change their meaning because they will evoke, between them, only a part rather than the whole of the available stereotyped economic arguments for fault and strict liability.

I think it probable that "she is the cheapest cost avoider" will disappear from the lexicon, rather than persisting until a new equilibrium is reached. But if the new bite does persist, it is not at all likely that it will do so without affecting the whole system. The analogy (present to the mind of Saussure when he developed this analysis at the turn of the century) is to the impact of the appearance of a new commodity on the prices of all other commodities in a Walrasian general equilibrium system.[1]

VI. Nesting

"Nesting" is my name for the reproduction, within a doctrinal solution to a problem, of the policy conflict the solution was supposed to settle. Take the case of killing in mistaken self-defense. In *Courvoisier v. Raymond*,[2] a shopkeeper shot and injured a person he thought was a looter emerging from a crowd of rioters. The person was in fact a policeman coming to his aid. In this fact situation, the courts have initially to decide whether there should be a defense of mistake in self-defense situations. A court taking up the question for the first time has to decide it in the context of considerable doctrinal conflict over when mistake is a defense to the commission of an intentional tort.

Some of the considerations commonly advanced in favor of and against the defense are:

> the shopkeeper shouldn't have to pay because he was not at fault
> vs.

the shopkeeper should pay because as between two innocents he who caused the damage should pay

people have a right to act in self-defense when they believe
they are in danger
vs.
people have a right to security of the person as they go
about their lawful business

imposing liability would discourage people from the desirable activity of self-defense
vs.
refusing to impose liability would discourage people from
assisting others in trouble

people expect to be able to defend themselves when they
feel they are in danger
vs.
people don't expect to be harmed arbitrarily

allowing mistake is an example of equitable flexibility in
imposing liability
vs.
the vagueness of a mistake standard will lead to uncertainty avoided by a rigid rule of compensation for deliberate
injury

there are many analogies for this defense
vs.
no court has recognized this defense before

deciding the precise contours of a mistake defense requires
input that only the legislature can command
vs.
courts do this kind of thing every day

Please resist the impulse to assess the strength of these arguments as they appear in this context. What we are concerned with is "nesting," a formal attribute of legal argument. Nesting occurs as follows. Let us suppose that the court accepts the argument in favor of a defense of mistake. It looks as though the defendant has won. But now suppose the plaintiff argues that the defendant's mistake was "unreasonable," meaning that a person of ordinary intelligence and caution would not have shot, under the circumstances, without more indication that he was in danger. Suppose the plaintiff concedes that the defendant acted in the good faith belief that he was in danger. Suppose the defendant in turn concedes he was less intelligent and cautious than the average man in the community.

In deciding whether reasonableness should matter, a court that has accepted the argument cast in the form above will consider a new version of the inventory:

> If the plaintiff acted in good faith, he was not at fault
> vs.
> as between two innocents, he who caused the damage should pay
>
> people are entitled to be judged according to their actual capabilities
> vs.
> people have a right to protection from the unreasonable behaviour of others
>
> an objective standard will deter people from defending themselves
> vs.
> a subjective standard will deter people from going to the aid of others
>
> a subjective standard will encourage people like the plaintiff to pay attention to the actual danger they face in helping out

vs.

a subjective standard will encourage carelessness by people contemplating self-defense

the community does not expect more of people in danger than that they act in good faith

vs.

the community expects people in danger to act reasonably

adjusting the standard to the actual character of the defendant allows equitable flexibility

vs.

a "subjective good faith" standard is hopelessly vague and manipulable

this is the first time the court has imposed a reasonableness limitation on the right of self-defense

vs.

reasonableness is the general rule in defining permissible conduct

"Nesting" is the reappearance of the inventory when we have to resolve gaps, conflicts or ambiguities that emerge when we try to put our initial solution to a doctrinal problem into practice. In this case, we first deploy the pro and con argument-bites in deciding whether or not to permit a defense of mistake. We then redeploy them in order to decide whether to require that the mistake be reasonable. In this case, the courts have in practice chosen to honour the pro-defendant arguments in creating the defense, but to honour the pro-plaintiff (reasonableness) arguments in defining its contours.

This situation can be represented visually as follows:

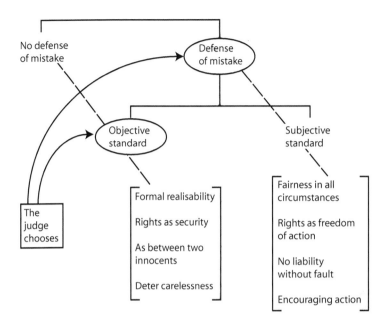

We might also represent the choice in terms of a continuum, as follows:

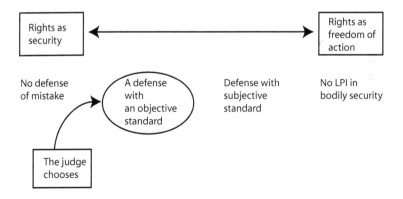

I would argue that this second representation in terms of a continuum conveys far less of the structure of legal argument than the nesting diagram, for two reasons.

First, practitioners of legal argument proceed, both within a given case and over a series of cases, from the more general choices to the more particular, arguing and then re-arguing, rather than debating the merits of a point on the continuum versus all the other points on the continuum. This, indeed, is one of the more powerful of all the conventions of legal argument.

Second, an equally powerful convention of legal argument is that argument and counter-argument are presented as simply "correct" as applied to the general question, without this presentation binding the arguer in any way on the nested sub-question. In other words, the judge can, without violating any norm of legal argument, state that "equitable flexibility is so important that it requires us to accept a defense of mistake here," and then turn around and state that "certainty is so important that we are obliged to reject a 'good faith' test in favor of reasonableness."

Of course, it may be true that what the judge is "really" doing is "balancing" the conflicting policy vectors to determine just that spot on the continuum where the benefit of certainty comes to outweigh the benefit of flexibility. Moreover, in some courts and in some doctrinal areas it is permissible for the judge to present the decision in this way. The nesting presentation is nonetheless privileged in argumentative practice.

My sense is that the reason for this is that the nesting presentation is associated with "objectivity." Judges prefer it because it harmonizes with the stereotypically judicial pole in the judge/legislator dichotomy. But that argument is for another place. For the moment, let me emphasize the general character of the nesting schema by offering another, much briefer example. In the case of *Vincent v. Lake Erie*,[3] a ship's captain chose to remain moored to a dock during a storm, and even reinforced his mooring lines, in spite of the fact that the ship's heaving against the dock was visibly damaging it. The question was whether the ship owner had to compensate the dock owner for the damage.

The nesting sequence begins with the question whether or not there should be a privilege of necessity. In other words, was the destruction of the dock a legal wrong? If it was, then in most cases it would follow not only that the ship-owner would have to compensate the dock owner for the damage, but also that the dock owner could, in self-defense, repel or unmoor the ship. The ship owner would possibly be subject to criminal penalties, and, time permitting, to an injunction against continuing in place, and, potentially, to liability for punitive damages.

If, on the other hand, the captain's action was privileged, none of these consequences would follow. Indeed, it would have been wrongful for the dock owner to unmoor the vessel. In the *Vincent* case, the court was clearly unwilling to subject the ship owner to civil or criminal penalties, or to an injunction that would have forced his departure (had circumstances permitted), or to unmooring by the dock owner. But the court held that the ship-owner had to pay the dock owner compensation, so that although the destruction of the dock was privileged, the privilege was "incomplete," rather than "absolute."

The arguments that courts and commentators advance in favor of a privilege of necessity are familiar from the previous exercise. They include ideas like "equitable flexibility," the absence of fault on the part of the captain, the right to self-preservation, the social desirability of preserving the more valuable piece of property, and so forth. In *Vincent,* these arguments prevailed on the issue whether the ship owner had acted criminally, would be enjoined, or would be made to pay punitive damages.

When courts and commentators consider the question of simple money compensation for the destruction of the dock, they redeploy the inventory. This time, they come down on the side of compensation, explaining themselves by adopting the rhetoric of certainty, as between two innocents, the right of security, and so forth, the very arguments they rejected when deciding the prior question. This can be represented as "nesting" or in continuum terms:

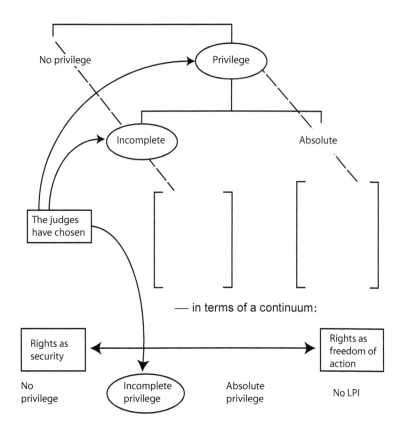

Nesting represents the conservation of argumentative energy. Within a given topic or cluster, there are far fewer arguments deployed than one would expect if one paid attention only to the seemingly endless variety of issues and sub-issues that arise. But nesting also represents the conservation of argument-bites. The play of bite and counter-bite settles nothing (except the case at hand). As between the bites themselves, every fight is a draw, and all combatants live to fight another day, neither discredited by association with the losing side nor established as correct by association with a winner. There are no killer arguments outside a particular context.

VII. Conclusion

Although the above is very tentative and obviously radically incomplete, I hope it is already apparent that it might be disquieting. In the introduction to this paper, I put this in the language of post-structuralism, for reasons that may be clearer at this point. The argument-bites I focused on (how typical?) are defined by their counter-bites. Legal argument has a certain mechanical quality, once one begins to identify its characteristic operations. Language seems to be "speaking the subject," rather than the reverse. It is hard to imagine that argument so firmly channeled into bites could reflect the full complexity either of the fact situation or of the decision-maker's ethical stance toward it. It is hard to imagine doing this kind of argument in utter good faith, that is, to imagine doing it without some cynical strategy in fitting foot to shoe. But I admit that these rather unconventional conclusions (unconventional within law, I mean) are only suggested by the above. The development of the linguistic analogy for legal argument may end up taking us in quite the opposite direction for all one can tell for sure at this point.

Appendix I: Methodological Origins of This Semiotics of Legal Argument

There is now a small but substantial literature that adopts the general approach to legal argument described in this paper.[4] And the more general post-modern approach to legal theory now has a literature too large to list fully.[5]

According to Jack Balkin,[6] the idea of discussing legal discourse as deployed in dyadic choices between possible legal rules was "borrowed from various Structuralist thinkers." In a footnote, he cites C. Levi-Strauss, *The Raw and the Cooked* (1969) and C. Levi-Strauss, *Structural Anthropology* (1963, 1976).[7] It is also a commonplace that critical legal studies approaches to legal reasoning are "just" a revival of legal realism.[8] Well, which is it?

It seems to me that the version of legal semiotics represented by this paper is a kind of jerry-built amalgam of elements from realism and structuralism, but not an "application" or "revival" of either. Though there is an element of fatheadedness in "tracing the origins of my thought," that is just what I'd like to do briefly in this appendix. My goal is not to settle the question of origins and influences (impossible to do in any case) but to contribute some raw material for the study of borrowing.

As I see it, there are three basic elements to the proposed semiotics of legal argument. These are: (1) the idea of reducing the "parole" of legal argument to a "langue" composed of argument-bites, (2) the idea of relating the bites to one another through "operations," and (3) the idea of "nesting," or the reproduction, in the application of a doctrinal formula, of the confrontation between argument-bites that the formula purported to resolve.

A. Argument-Bites

The first idea, like the other two, was probably occurring to a lot of different people at more or less the same time. For me, it was a way to radicalize, for the purposes of a law school paper debunking "policy argument" in constitutional law, Llewellyn's famous article *Canons on Statutes*, which was reprinted as an appendix to *The Common Law Tradition: Deciding Appeals.*[9] Llewellyn had no interest in extending his critique of statutory interpretation to legal reasoning in general. The realists as a group were more preoccupied with the critique of what they saw as formalist argumentative techniques than they were with reflection on their own beloved alternative of policy analysis.

The extension of the "bites" analysis from statutory interpretation to policy discourse meant rejecting the "reconstructive" impulse among the realists, which seemed (in 1970) to be an evasion of the more "irrationalist" or "existential" implications of their own work. Policy discourse at the time seemed deeply implicated in, indeed the major vehicle of the Cold War Liberalism against which the anti-war movement, the civil rights movement and the women's movement were then aligning themselves.

The source in structuralism of the idea of reducing legal argument to bites was Levi-Strauss's discussion of "bricolage" in the first chapter of *The Savage Mind*.[10] Levi-Strauss relativizes the distinction between rationality, or technical reasoning, and the activity of myth making. In spite of its pretensions to fit precisely whatever phenomenon it addresses, technical reasoning is inevitably the "jerry-building" (bricolage) of an edifice out of elements borrowed from here and there, elements initially meant for other purposes (and themselves therefore jerry-built of yet other, earlier bits and pieces). Legal argument, understood as the deployment of stereotyped pro and con argument fragments, seems a particularly good example of bricolage masquerading as hyper-rationality.

At first, this idea seemed useful mainly for classroom teaching. It was the basis for "mantras" of argument and counter-argument about contract formalities, for example. I used it, tentatively, in *Form and Substance in Private Law Adjudication*,[11] in developing the stereotyped pro-con exchange of arguments about the choice between rules and standards, and in a discussion of the problem of the conflict of rights in *The Structure of Blackstone's Commentaries*.[12] When I switched to teaching torts, I incorporated it into teaching materials, beginning with what then seemed the pair of pairs: no liability without fault vs. as between two innocents.

This article attempts a further incorporation of structuralist ideas by recasting the "canons" analysis of argument-bites in the terms of F. Saussure, *Course in General Linguistics*.[13] This represents a circuitous return to origins, since the idea of bricolage was itself an adaptation of the Saussurian theory of the sign.[14] I'm sure there are disadvantages to assimilating legal argument to the general analysis of signs. But the move seems to make available for legal semiotics many insights of the more general study that will advance the specifically legal enterprise.

It is a problem that discussions of Saussurian linguistics in the American intellectual community often make it sound as though signs "get their meaning from each other" in a way that utterly divorces them from their referents, indeed in a way that suggests that they "signify" nothing but their relations among themselves. In the "Concluding Remark on the Interdependence of the Meanings of Argument-Bites," in the text, I propose a much less metaphysical rendering of Saussure's insight.

B. Operations

The second element in the proposed semiotics of legal argument is the notion of an "operation." Jack Balkin is right in associating this idea with Hohfeld.[15] When Hohfeld pointed out the ambiguity in the common legal usage of the word "right," that it sometimes meant "privilege" and sometimes "claim," he suggested the possibility of answering every privilege-assertion with a claim-assertion.[16] This seems to me the prototypical operation.[17]

A second realist origin is in the early twentieth-century debate about the social utility of more or less extensive protection of intangible property rights. Holmes's dissent in the *Northern Securities* case,[18] along with his concurring opinion in *International News Service v. Associated Press*,[19] Learned Hand's opinion in *Cheney v. Doris Silk* Co.,[20] and Chafee's article, *Unfair Competition*,[21] suggest a formal procedure for generating utilitarian "pro-property" and "pro-competition" arguments in any antitrust or unfair competition case.[22]

The structuralist element in the theory of operations was borrowed from J. Piaget, *Six Psychological Essays*.[23] Until recently, it has seemed to me that the main value of Piaget's work for legal analysis lies in his theory of "accommodation" and "assimilation" in the development of "schemas."[24] A number of us have used these or roughly equivalent ideas from other sources in trying to work out a picture of the historical transformations of American legal "consciousness."[25] A second use of the Piagetian approach is in trying to understand how judges decide cases by "assimilating" or recasting the facts to fit the legal materials that exist at a given moment, while "accommodating" or recasting the materials to fit the irreducible particularity of the facts.[26]

This essay extends the Piagetian notion of a schema to legal argument about the choice between two possible rules or between two interpretations of a rule. Arguing about a choice is like sucking or shaking an object: it is an acquired cognitive procedure, a "praxis," a pre-structured "response" to a "stimulus." The stimulus is the demand for justification of an outcome. The structured response, in this model, is an argument for a rule, or for an interpretation of a rule, that will produce that outcome.

The goal is to catalogue the particular "operations" through which an arguer moves among argument-bites to construct the case for an outcome. The focus is on the identification of the very particular schemas linking one argument-bite with another. The crucial Piagetian concept here is that of "reversibility" of schemas.[27] When an arguer has attained the capacity to move from any bite to all others associated with it, and back again, he or she can, first, build an argument's initial rough draft simply by reaction to the opponent's formulation of his case, second, anticipate an opponent's argument simply by examining what she herself will say, and, third, carry on an internal version of the argument playing both parts.

On a quite different level, the experience of legal argument as operations defines the "tone" of modern legal consciousness, the loss of the sense of the organic or unmediated in legal thought.

As with the adoption of a Saussurian framework, reliance on Piaget has its dangers. It is common in the American intellectual community to think "Piaget is a structuralist," and that "therefore" he believes (1) that particular schemas and operations are innate, and (2) that "the structures determine what people think and do."

First, the borrowing of Piagetian formalizations of the phenomena of reasoning (schema, accommodation, assimilation, operation, reversibility) does not at all imply borrowing whatever theory Piaget holds about their proper interpretation. While the biological status of "conservation of the object" is a tough question, it would be absurd to argue that either "no liability without fault" or "as between two innocents" is either innate or what "determines" an outcome.

Piaget's work on moral reasoning would appear to be the most relevant to legal reasoning, because Piaget there adapted his cognitive psychology to purposes not unlike ours here.[28] But his stage theory of moral development is about as far as one can get from the approach of this paper. The idea of "justice" toward which he sees children tending seems no more than a hodgepodge, an inadequately analysed combination of cooperation, consent, autonomy, mutual respect and "reason."[29] He seems obtuse about the "operational" character of moral argument that his own work on cognition suggests. The adoption of the Saussurian framework represents for me the rejection of the notions that arguments determine outcomes by being correct (within the framework of a particular stage), and that there is a privileged or "highest" mode of argument.

Second, the common American understanding of Piaget's structuralism as a determinism analogous, say, to orthodox Marxism or socio-biology in social theory, or to orthodox Freudianism or behaviourism in psychology, is a misunderstanding. He seems most open to that charge when he is closest to discussing justice,[30] but this is where he is least useful to lawyers. As a cognitive psychologist, he seems closer to Levi-Strauss, for whom some structure is always given, but given as langue rather than as parole, and always changing.

C. Nesting

The third element in the proposed semiotics of legal argument is "nesting," or the reproduction of particular argumentative oppositions within the doctrinal structures that apparently resolve them. This idea owes a lot to the basic realist pedagogical technique of presenting the student with a series of hypotheticals that cause him or her to produce contradictory arguments over a sequence of cases. But I also borrowed it quite directly from C. Levi-Strauss's *The Savage Mind*,[31] in the ambiguous mode of bricolage.

There are three relevant notions, each with a nesting diagram, in *The Savage Mind*. The first[32] is that the elements of a system of plant classification are arranged in oppositions that correspond to social divisions and practices. These oppositions are sometimes used and reused according to a nesting pattern. His example is the use of *Chrysothamnus* as a signifier of maleness in opposition to *Artemisia* (sagebrush), signifying the feminine. The Navaho (according to Levi-Strauss) employ this general North American system, but also categorize *Chrysothamnus* as a feminine plant because it is used in assisting childbirth. He explains the "logic" of the system as follows:

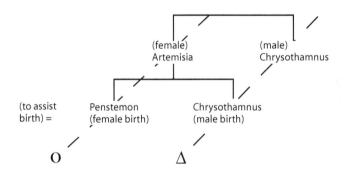

Chrysothamnus is male in the "main opposition," and plays the male role when it is reemployed within the female division. This synchronic presentation contrasts with a later exploration of the diachronics of structures.[33] Levi-Strauss discusses how the structure we see may be unintelligible without understanding its history. He imagines a tribe divided into three clans, with each name symbolizing an element:

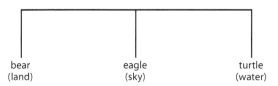

He continues: "suppose further that demographic changes led to the extinction of the bear clan and an increase in the population of the turtle clan, and that as a result the turtle clan split into two sub-clans, each of which subsequently gained the status of clans. The old structure will disappear completely, and be replaced by a structure of this type:"

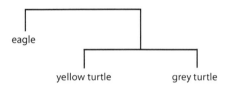

Levi-Strauss speculates that "after this upheaval the three clan names might survive only as traditionally accepted titles with no cosmological significance." But it is also possible that the tribe will understand what has happened as a "logical" transformation of the original system. The new scheme might be intelligible because "there were originally three terms, and the number of terms is still the same at the end. The original three terms expressed an irreducible trichotomy while the final three terms are the result of two successive dichotomies; between sky and water and then between yellow and grey."[34]

Then comes what seemed to me the punch line: "It can be seen therefore that demographic evolution can shatter the structure but that if the structural orientation survives the shock it has, after each upheaval several means of re-establishing a system, which may not be identical with the earlier one but is at least formally of the same type."[35]

A third suggestive passage contrasts endogamy with exogamy. According to Levi-Strauss, exogamous systems practice either "restricted" or "generalized" exchange, with the former indicating that marriage partners for group A must be from group B, but not from groups C, D, etc. This leads to the following diagram:

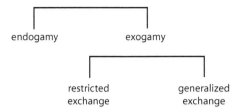

Levi-Strauss comments: "It will be seen that restricted exchange, the 'closed' form of exogamy, is logically closer to endogamy than the 'open' form, generalized exchange."[36]

Back to law. It seemed to me, as an amateur left-wing jurisprude in 1970, that the Hart & Sacks *Legal Process* materials of 1958 represented the current liberal orthodoxy, and played a role in legitimating the passive response of academics and judges to the "crises of the time." In a paper critiquing those materials, I argued that they were but the latest in a succession of responses to attacks on the distinction between legislation and adjudication. Each attack had managed to discredit an earlier version of the distinction, but had led to a new version of similar structure. My diagram was utterly contextual, but turned out (to my surprise and delight) to look very like the Levi-Strauss prototypes described above:

Transformation of Utopian Rationalist Thought

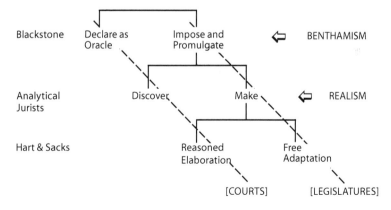

There are several steps between this and the classroom diagrams of *Courvoisier v. Raymond* and *Vincent v. Lake Erie*. I won't try to work them out here.[37] Nesting is first of all something that happens, a phenomenon. It is also quite mysterious, and needs further study and interpretation.[38] I admit to a prejudice in favor of trying to "discover" things like this, as opposed to elaborating internally the realist or structuralist (or whatever) paradigms on whose intermixing discovery seems to be dependent.

Appendix II: Responses to Four European Objections

Although *A Semiotics of Legal Argument*, to which this is a European Appendix, was written for an American audience, it is shamelessly European-theoretical in its approach. It is an attempt to summarize and extend one of the innovations of American critical legal studies — the appropriation for the analysis of legal argument of the structuralism of Saussure, Levi-Strauss and Piaget. The American introduction gives a post-modern, specifically Derridian, gloss to the enterprise.

In the article, I identify what I claim are the stereotyped "argument-bites" that legal reasoners use when the legal issue is one that permits a reference to the policies or purposes or underlying objectives of the legal order, rather than a legal issue that can be satisfactorily resolved through deductive rule application or by reference to binding precedent. It is crucial to understanding the article that it is about the choice between two definitions of an ambiguous rule, or between two possible solutions to a gap between rules, or between two conflicting rules. It is not about the application of rules to facts.

Thus, what we have appropriated these famous Europeans for is the American project of radicalizing legal realism. It is striking that European legal scholars, while recognizing them as among the most brilliant, formative characters in their own intellectual tradition, have found no similar use for their work. I think this phenomenon is a key to many interesting current contrasts between European and American legal culture. Here I mean to work on this comparative law question only indirectly, by taking up four objections that Europeans I know have made to the particular appropriation of structuralism and post-modernism that this article represents. I think brief responses to the objections may be a helpful first step in the long-run project. The four objections are:

(A) in Europe, the policy arguments I identify are not present, at least not in the stereotyped form that I claim they take in American legal materials;

(B) as a theory of law, this is just "law is rhetoric," well known since the sophists, revived by Perelman, easily refuted by the fact of frequent legal determinacy;

(C) as a theory of law, this is just "no rule can determine the scope of its own application," well known since Wittgenstein, obvious to anyone who has read Derrida;

(D) European law is so much more formal, certain and legislative than American that the analysis of mere policy argument is of little use East of the Big Water.

A. The Arguments Identified are Not Present as Stereotyped Bites in European Legal Argumentative Practice

I have not read enough European legal arguments, whether in opinions, briefs or arguments of public counsel to be able to respond directly to this objection. But it does seem clear that European lawyers in casual discussion of legal issues use exactly the same argument-bites as do Americans. Moreover, the initial task of generalizing and formalizing legal policy argument was a joint project of German and French scholars (for example, Jhering and Demogue). While leaving open the possibility that policy argument in Europe does not have the stereotypical character that I allege is present in the US, I am skeptical.

My sense is that Europeans do not recognize the bites that I isolate in this article because they are unfamiliar with the analysis of policy argument as a practice. Paradoxically, the characteristic European alternation between a cynical and a formalist legal consciousness enables them to do policy argument unselfconsciously, from "the inside," as though each argument were a tailor-made response to "the facts." In cynical legal consciousness, argument is experienced as transparently manipulative and instrumental, reflecting the pre-selected partisan interest of the arguer. In the formalist mode, there is an uncritical acceptance of whatever the judge says as authoritative. Policy argument, which is above all a mediation between partisan or ideological interest and legal logic and universality, doesn't figure on either side of the cynicism/formalism divide.

In the American mode, there is a much larger intermediate area within which neither cynicism nor formalism, but a vague natural law or normative consciousness prevails. I should say that I consider this American mode to be alternately naive and self-serving; I do not think it represents a viable "third space" between freedom and mechanical constraint. The effort to develop it, however, has led to a kind of self-consciousness about the normative enterprise in law that is lacking in Europe.

I have a sense that this difference between cultures is gradually lessening, in part because of the general phenomenon of American cultural imperialism in law, but in larger part because the development of the law of the European Community has occurred in a fashion strikingly similar to the development of American law. But more of this in the discussion of the fourth objection.

B. The Bites Analysis is Just Another Example of the Theory that Law is Rhetoric

The notion here is that at least since the sophists there has existed a "nihilist" strand in legal philosophy that denies the "objective" status of legal reasoning, claiming that it is always possible to argue either side of a legal issue and that the arguments come in stereotyped form as "topoi." Is "this" just "that"? There is an undeniable link between the approach of this article and that tradition, although the actual influence of Perelman's rhetoric theory is indirect (the rhetoric theory influenced at least a few legal realists, for example, Friedrich Kessler, and thereby critical legal studies).

But there are also important differences between the rhetoric theory and the approach taken here. First, I am not proposing a "theory of law" in the familiar European legal philosophical sense (positivism, natural law, Scandinavian realism, etc.). This article is a description of the practice of policy argument, understood as one of the many activities of lawyers, judges and legislators. I think of it as a contribution to the positive sociology of legal knowledge.

Second, I don't deny that there is often an experience of determination of the outcome of a legal case by a single, obviously applicable, pre-existing rule, so that resort to policy argument appears unnecessary or even improper. I make no general assertion that law is always indeterminate, or that it is always possible to argue both sides of a question. As a matter of fact, the contrary is quite obviously the case — as a matter of fact, it is not always possible to argue both sides.

At the same time, it is uncontroversial that rule systems contain gaps, conflicts and ambiguities that arguers routinely present as resolved by appeal to non-deductive legal reasons, or what I call, broadly, policy arguments (meaning to include arguments from principles and rights as well as instrumental or consequentialist arguments), as opposed to being resolved by the deductive procedure of rule application. In other words, there is a second experience of legal necessity, different from that of deductive rule application. What is controversial, in legal philosophy, is how to understand this doubleness of the phenomenon of legal necessity.

There are a number of questions here. This article addresses one of them: With what tools do legal arguers generate the experience of necessity in cases that appear to require, for their resolution, something more than the deductive application of rule to facts? In other words, this article is about the choice among possible definitions for the rule applicable to the facts, a choice made necessary by the existence of gaps, conflicts and ambiguities. Given the experience of non-deductive determinacy, this can be understood as a kind of base line, or fundamental question for the sociology of legal knowledge. I see it as only one part of the general study of the experience of a legal judgment as legally necessary. (In the positivist tradition, the necessity in question is normative only to the degree that on some independent basis there is a moral obligation to obey the law. Whether or not there is such an obligation, necessity means that there is a non-deductive "correct," "objectively required," legal outcome to the problem of rule-definition.)

I undertake the inquiry into the practice of non-deductive legal argument about rule-definition without any pre-commitments as to the ontological status of the necessity that legal arguers sometimes achieve for themselves and their audience. I treat the factual experience of necessity, very much in the post-modern mode, as an "effect." This means rigorously constraining oneself to the structural analysis of the textual productions of the arguers, and ignoring their own claims about the ontological status of the necessity they produce — that is, their claims about how their arguments reflect the "truth" about the positively enacted legal materials or about the logic of legal reasoning (or the two combined). The study of the effect of necessity thus means making a very traditional Continental maneuver — that of "bracketing," or simply putting aside for the time being or maybe forever, the question of the "essence" of which necessity might be an "appearance," and concentrating instead on the "phenomenology" of necessity. Judith Butler has recently adopted a similar approach to the phenomenon of gender identity.

The analysis of the production of legal necessity in legal texts is quite different from the analysis of the production of moral or political-philosophical necessity in discussions of what the law ought to be. (Because in moral or political-philosophical argument there are other sources of normative authority than the rule of recognition, and because any given legal system is likely to exclude categorically some moral and political arguments.) But one might choose to explore the current practice of normative argument in legal philosophy using the same bracketing technique this article applies to positive legal argument.

From the point of view of the normative theorists themselves, such an inquiry would be strictly speaking irrelevant, or, I would say more optimistically, strictly speaking preliminary to normative legal philosophy conceived as the search for a grounding (a normative "behind") for legal judgment. But the inquiry is irrelevant or preliminary not because it is "just" a rhetoric theory or because it is "nihilist," but because it is not about normative judgment.

Analyzing the structure of legal argument does not help us figure out what the rule or its application should be as a matter of principle, or if we took rights seriously, or in the ideal speech situation; it even more clearly does not help us figure out whether the notions of principle or of rights or of an ideal speech situation are coherent. (I doubt they are.) The strategy here is based on the idea that the investigation of the effect or phenomenon of legal necessity is "interesting" in the short run and likely to have an indirect impact on our normative thinking in the long run.

The study of non-deductive legal argument about rule-definition, in the mode of this article, seems to produce, quite often, an experience of disillusionment akin to that of "loss of faith" in the religious domain. It is not that the stereotyped and mechanically operational character of non-deductive legal discourse "proves" anything at all about the possibility of moral grounding. It is just that a large proportion of moral and political-philosophical discourse seems to be a somewhat elaborated version of the legal argument-bites, no less stereotypical and no more self-conscious about the problem of interminable operational transformability. On this reading, the normative legal philosophers have underestimated the challenge of skepticism, perhaps because they have relied on unsophisticated pictures of how law works.

The attempt to plumb the normative "behind" has been consistently distorted by reliance on particular understandings of the "surface" or illusory present of legal argument. What is particular about these understandings is sometimes their reliance on common sense or culturally current notions about law that are obviously part of the self-serving ideology of the legal profession. But what is particular is also sometimes the circular derivation of the analysis of the illusory present or surface of legal argument from the very "meta" commitments (to conceptions of the "nature" of law or legal determinacy) that the descriptions supposedly validate.

C. No Rule Can Determine the Scope of its Own Application

The third objection is that the insight that policy analysis cannot determine rule-definition is uninteresting, because it follows from the well-known point that no rule can determine the scope of its own application. If rules cannot determine outcomes, it would be naive to expect policy arguments to determine rules. A variant of this critique is sometimes stated in post-modernist terms: difference or slippage between the textually affirmed determinacy of the rule as signifier and the signified—a particular instance of rule application—is inevitable. That this should be true of rule-choice as well as of rule application is no surprise.

A first response is that this article does not attempt to establish that policy analysis (broadly conceived) can or can't do anything. It describes how policy analysis works in practice—that is, what its textual content is and how practitioners manipulate it by operating on the elements of that given content. As a matter of fact, it appears that practitioners sometimes use policy argument to generate in their audience the experience of the necessity of a particular choice of rule definition. But this article does no more than describe the tools with which they sometimes succeed and sometimes fail at this task.

The article is also part of a broader attempt at a positive sociology of legal knowledge. The broader goal is to understand how two social practices, norm definition and adjudication "under" norms, fit into and affect social life. No one seems to think we should jump from the logically impeccable assertion that no rule can determine the scope of its own application to the conclusion that these practices, of positive enactment and adjudication, are irrelevant to understanding what happens in society until we know what does determine the scope of their application, if indeed that can ever be known.

But neither the Wittgensteinian nor the post-modern way of understanding the maxim is much help, at least as of now, in trying to do sociology in the aftermath of the loss of faith in rules as self-applying. In its logical, or Wittgensteinian form, as a proposition about rules, the problem is that the maxim's truth is merely negative, no help in explaining the actual experience of the organization of action through rules. Within that approach, it is common to resort to the notion of a form of life, or interpretive community.

But the assertion of the existence of some mode of intersubjectivity that permits rules to work is no more than the insertion of a "black box." We still have to figure out how "interpretive communities" come into existence and how they function to make both rule application and the resolution of gaps, conflicts and ambiguities possible. This is exactly the level at which the study of non-deductive legal argument becomes a necessity, since it is one of the conspicuous elements of the actual practice of interpretive community.

In the alternative post-modern version, it is wrong to interpret "difference" as a logically necessary aspect of interpretation—it is merely an event that sometimes subverts the aspiration to presence through textuality. To elevate it to a logical necessity—to treat it as something inevitable, a "truth"—would land us in the aporetically self-invalidating position of affirming the truth of the impossibility of truth, while at the same time denying the actual experience of determinacy. Deconstruction is rather an event brought about by someone doing the work of deconstruction; whether it will "happen" in any given case cannot be known in advance, no matter how sure the deconstructer may feel that he or she will succeed.

At this point, the study of the structure of non-deductive legal argument is useful not as a way to instantiate or to endlessly re-prove the truth of the maxim, but as part of the post- or pre-post-modern enterprise of figuring out how the experience of necessity can come into being in the world and yet succumb, endlessly, to undermining.

There are numerous puzzles here. First, if no rule can determine the scope of its own application, what are we to make of the experience of deduction: there sometimes seems to be only one possibly relevant rule, the scope of whose application *seems* to be determined straightforwardly—by applying the definitions of the terms of the rule to facts that have themselves been authoritatively formulated so that they fit the definitions? When this happens, as, let's face it, it does all the time, what is going on? Is the experience always rightly characterized as making a mistake about the truth of the situation?

Legal work can often destabilize the experience of a given case as involving only issues of rule application, in effect generating a gap, conflict or ambiguity where none at first appeared. On the other hand, legal work can often at least apparently resolve into legal necessity a gap, conflict or ambiguity that had at first appeared to require some kind of extra-juristic basis for decision. When these things happen, are we to understand them as a process of discovery of an underlying, trans-argumentative reality about the legal materials, or as "ungrounded?"

This article has nothing to say about these questions. It is about the structure of the practice of non-deductive legal argument. Nonetheless, it poses a challenge for those who believe that there is a form of non-deductive legal necessity, necessity in the choice of a rule definition in the face of a gap, conflict or ambiguity, that is something more than the brute experience of not being able to come up with a plausible counter to a proposed legal solution. But the challenge is not in the form of a logical refutation, not direct in the way that "no rule can determine the scope of its own application" confronts naive theories of ordering through rules.

The challenge is this: Given the stereotyped content of the argumentative repertoire, and the operational practices by which the repertoire is adapted to particular situations, by what mechanism can we imagine non-deductive legal necessity in rule-definition coming into being?

D. The Analysis of Policy Argument is Irrelevant for Europe Because European Law is Formal, Certain and Legislative by Contrast with American Law

The fourth objection is that the kind of policy argument this article describes counts for a lot in the United States (and perhaps in Anglo-Commonwealth countries other than Britain), but not because it has to in the nature of legal reasoning. American culture is notably informal by contrast with European. It is "freer," in some very desirable senses, but always bordering on *laissez aller*, unbuttoned, without underlying structures of educational, cultural and social discipline.

American law is particularly uncertain, both because of its precedential (as opposed to code) basis and because of federalism. In interpreting a legal corpus that is already notably uncertain, American judges have shown themselves incapable of being, or unwilling to be bound by the elements of formality that do exist in the system. They substitute policy analysis for the missing elements of codification and strict adherence to legal logic. In the process, they arrogate to themselves, and are conceded, a degree of power far greater than would be tolerated in Europe, where it is taken for granted that codes combined with the discipline of legal reasoning subordinate them to legislative authority.

The result is a kind of vicious circle, in which uncertainty in an already informal general culture invites policy analytic approaches that allow judges to usurp the legislative function, which in turn accentuates uncertainty, inviting further policy analysis, and so on. It is not surprising that American scholars are obsessed with determinacy and indeterminacy in adjudication, but it is also not very interesting for Europeans.

Is this at all plausible? What about the alternative theory, that European legal culture is simply undeveloped by contrast with

American? Perhaps Europeans do indeed experience legal necessity in situations where Americans see gaps, conflicts and ambiguities arbitrarily rather than rationally resolved. But perhaps the explanation is not the European code system, or unitary national states, or greater mastery of or cultural commitment to the forms of legal reasoning, but innocence, paradoxical willed innocence, for better or worse, of the possibility of non-Marxist legal critique.

If this is the case, the development of the law of the European Community poses already and will continue to pose a profound challenge to the strategic denial of the nature of adjudication. Moreover, the objective, or more broadly the merely rational character of adjudication, its capacity to generate the effect of necessity, is an important building block in the construction of Western culture. Legal necessity is a model for necessity in general (not, of course, the only model). For this reason, the challenge is to something more than the role of judges in European integration or disintegration. This is not the place to explore these questions, beyond the remark that the exclusion from influence on European legal scholarship of the most advanced European critical thinkers in the structuralist and post-modern traditions may be more than an accident. It may be one of the mechanisms through which the undeveloped reconstitutes itself as the merely conservative.

Notes

1. F. De Saussure, *Course in General Linguistics* (R. Hams trans. 1986) 112-14.

2. 23 Colorado Reports 113, 47 Pacific Reporter 284 (1896).

3. 109 Minnesota Reports 456, 125 Northern Western Reporter 221 (1910).

4. The contributions I am aware of are: D. Kennedy, *International Legal Structures* (1987); Bakkan, "Constitutional Arguments: Interpretation and Legitimacy in Canadian Constitutional Thought," 27 *Osgoode Hall Law Journal* (1989) 123; Boyle, "The Anatomy of a Torts Class," 34 *American University Law Review* (1985) 1003; Frug, "The Ideology of Bureaucracy in American Law," 97 *Harv. L. Rev.* (1984) 1276; Gordon, "Unfreezing Le-gal Reality: Critical Approaches to Law," 15 *Florida University Law Review* (1987) 195; Heidt, "Recasting Behavior: An Essay for Beginning Law Students," 49 *University of Pittsburg Law Review* (1988) 1065; Jaff, "Frame-shifting: An Empowering Methodology for Teaching and Learning Legal Reasoning," 36 *Journal of Legal Education* (1986) 249; Kelman, "Interpretive Construction in the Criminal Law," 33 *Stanford Law Review* (1981) 591; Paul, "A Bedtime Story," 74 *Virginia Law Review* (1988) 915; Schlag, "Cannibal Moves, An Essay on the Metamorphoses of the Legal Distinction," 40 *Stanford Law Review* (1988) 92; Schlag, "Rules and Standards," 33 *UCLA Law Review* (1985) 379. The most complete presentation of the basic ideas in the field, and of the canonical examples, is Balkin, "The Crystalline Structure of Legal Thought," 39 *Rutgers Law Review* (1986) 1. *See also* Balkin, "Taking Ideology Seriously: Ronald Dworkin and the CLS Critique," 55 *UMKC Law Review* (1987) 392; Balkin, "Nested Oppositions," 99 *Yale Law Journal* (1990) 1669; Balkin, "The Hohfeldian Approach to Law and Semiotics," in R. Kevelson (ed.) 3 *Law & Semiotics* (1989) 31.

5. The works that I"ve read that are closest in inspiration to this essay are: M. Kramer, Legal Theory, Political Theory, and Deconstruction: Against Rhadamanthus (1991); Ashe, "Zig-zag Stitching and the Seamless Web: Thoughts on Reproduction and the Law," 13 *Nova Law Journal* (1989) 355; Balkin, "Deconstructive Practice and Legal Theory," 96 *Yale Law Journal* (1987) 743; Berman, "Sovereignty in Abeyance: Self-Determination and International Law," 7 *Wisconsin International*

Law Journal (1988) 51; Boyle, "The Politics of Reason: Critical Legal Studies and Local Social Thought," 133 *U. Pa Law Review* (1985) 684; Crenshaw, "Demarginalizing the Intersection of Race and Sex: A Black Feminist Critique of Antidiscrimination Doctrine, Feminist Theory and Antiracist Politics," *Chicago Legal Forum* (1989) 139; Dalton, "An Essay in the Deconstruction of Contract Doctrine," 94 *Yale Law Journal* (1985) 997; Frug, "Argument as Character," 40 *Stanford Law Review* (1988) 869 ; Frug, "Rereading Contracts: A Feminist Analysis of a Contracts Casebook," 34 *American University Law Review* (1985) 1065; Heller, "Structuralism and Critique," 36 *Stanford Law Review* (1984) 127; Kennedy, "Critical Theory, Structuralism and Contemporary Legal Scholarship," 21 *New England Law Review* (1986) 209; Kennedy, "The Turn to Interpretation," 58 *Southern California Law Review* (1985) 1; Kennedy, "Spring Break," 63 *Texas Law Review* (1985) 1277; Olsen, "The Sex of Law," D. Kairys (ed.), *The Politics of Law* (2nd ed., 1990); Peller, "The Metaphysics of American Law," 73 *California Law Review* (1985) 1152; Schlag, ""Le Hors de Texte, C"est Moi": The Politics of Form and the Domestication of Deconstruction," 11 *Cardozo Law Review* (1990) 1631; Torres & Milun, "Translating Yonnondio by Precedent and Evidence: The Mashpee Indian Case," *Duke Law Journal* (1990) 624. *But see also* Cardozo Law Review Symposium on Deconstruction and the Possibility of Justice (1990); W. Mitchell (ed.), The Politics of Interpretation (1983); M. Minow, Making All the Difference (1990). The longer this list got, the more arbitrary it began to seem. I am not suggesting a canon, and have only read a part of the literature.

6. "The Crystalline Structure of Legal Thought," 39 *Rutgers Law Review* (1986) 1, 5 n.9.

7. *See also* Balkin, *supra* note 4, at 40-41, and Balkin, "The Domestication of Law and Literature," 14 *Law and Society Inquiry* (1989) 787, 806 n.24 .

8. E.g., Duxbury, "Robert Hale and The Economy of Legal Force," 53 *MLR* (1990) 421.

9. K. Llewellyn, The Common Law Tradition: Deciding Appeals (1960) 521-35.

10. C. Levi-Strauss, *The Savage Mind* (1966) 16-22 (hot book in 1970).

11. Kennedy, "Form and Substance in Private Law Adjudication," 89 *Harv. L. Rev.* (1976) 1685.

12. Kennedy, "The Structure of Blackstone"s Commentaries," 28 *Buffalo Law Review* (1979) 205, 355-60.

13. F. Saussure, *Course in General Linguistics* (1916, R. Hams trans. 1986) (hot book for me in the Spring of 1989).

14. *See* Levi-Strauss, *supra* note 10, at 18.

15. *See* Balkin, *supra* note 4, at 32-35.

16. Hohfeld, Fundamental Conceptions as Applied in Legal Reasoning and Other Essays (1923).

17. *See* Kennedy & Michelman, "Are Property and Contract Efficient?," 8 *Hofstra Law Review* (1980) 711; Singer, "The Legal Rights Debate in Analytical Jurisprudence, from Bentham to Hohfeld," *Wisconsin Law Review* (1982) 975.

18. *Northern Sec. v. United States*, 193 U.S. 197 (1904) (Holmes, J., dissenting).

19. 248 U.S. 215 (Holmes, J., concurring).

20. 35 F.2d 279 (2d Cir. 1929).

21. Chafee; "Unfair Competition," 53 *Harv. L. Rev.* (1940) 1289.

22. *See* Peritz, "The "Rule of Reason" in Antitrust: Property Logic in Restraint of Competition," 40 *Hastings Law Review* (1989) 285; Rogers, "The Right of Publicity: Resurgence of Legal Formalism and Judicial Disregard of Policy Issues," 16 *Beverly Hills Bar Association Journal* (1982) 65.

23. J. Piaget, *Six Psychological Essays* (D. Elkin (ed.) 1967) 130-31.

24. *See* J. Piaget, Play, *Dreams and Imitation in Childhood* (C. Gattegno & F. Hodgson trans. 1962). *See also* J. Piaget, *The Child and Reality* (1976) 63-71.

25. See W. Forbath, Law and the Shaping of the American Labor Movement (1991); H. Hartog,The Public Property and Private Power: The Corporation of the City of New York in American Law (1983) 1730-1870; M. Horwitz, The Transformation of American Law (1977) 1780-1860; R. Steinfeld, The Disappearance of Indentured Servitude and the Invention of Free Labor in the United Slates (1991); M. Tushnet, The American Law of Slavery, 1810-1860: Considerations of Humanity and Interest (1981); Alexander, "The Dead Hand and the Law of Trusts in the 19th Century," 37; Stanford Law Review (1985) 1189; Alexander, "The Transformation of Trusts as a Legal Category, 1800-1914," 5 Law & History Review (1987) 303; Casebeer, "Teaching an Old Dog Old

Tricks: Coppage v. Kansas and At-Will Employment Revisited,"
6 Cardozo Law Review (1985) 765; Fineman & Gabel, "Contract
Law as Ideology," in D. Kairys (ed.), The Politics of Law: A Progressive Critique (2nd ed., 1990); Fisher, "Ideology, Religion and
the Constitutional Protection of Private Property: 1760-1860," 39
Emory Law Journal (1990) 65; Freeman, "Legitimizing Racial Discrimination through Anti-Discrimination Law," 62 Minnesota Law
Review (1978) 1049; Frug, "The City as a Legal Concept," 93 Harv.
L. Rev. (1980) 1057; Gordon, "Legal Thought and Legal Practice
in the Age of American Enterprise, 1870-1920," in G. Geison (ed.),
Professions And Professional Ideologies In America (1983) 70-110;
Gordon, "Critical Legal Histories," 36 Stanford Law Review (1985)
57; Hager, "Bodies Politic: The Progressive history of Organization-
al "Real Entity" Theory," 50 University of Pittsburg Law Review
(1989) 575; Hurvitz, "American Labor Law and the Doctrine of
Entrepreneurial Property Rights: Boycotts, Courts and the Juridi-
cal Reorientation of 1886-1895," 8 Industrial Relations Law Journal
(1986) 307; Jacobson, "The Private Use of Public Authority: Sovereignty and Associations in the Common Law," 29 Buffalo Law
Review (1980) 599; Kainen, "Nineteenth Century Interpretations
of the Federal Contract Clause: The Transformation from Vested
to Substantive Rights Against the State," 31 Buffalo Law Review
(1982) 381; Katz, "Studies in Boundary Theory: Three Essays in
Adjudication and Politics," 28 Buffalo Law Review (1979) 383;
Kelman, "American Labor Law and Legal Formalism: How "Legal
Logic" Shaped and Vitiated the Rights of American Workers," 58
St. John"s Law Review (1983) 1; Kennedy, "Primitive Legal Scholarship," 27 Harv. Int"l L.J. (1986) 1; Kennedy, "Toward an Historical Under-standing of Legal Consciousness: The Case of Classical
Legal Thought, 1850-1940," in J. Spitzer (ed.), Current Research
in the Sociology of Law (1980) Vol. 3; Kennedy, supra note 12; Kennedy, "The Role of Law in Economic Thought: Essays on Fetishism
of Commodities," 34 American University Law Review (1985) 939;
Klare, "The Deradicalization of the Wagner Act and the Origins of
Modern Legal Consciousness, 1937-1941," 62 Minnesota Law Review (1978) 265; Krauss, "On the Distinction Between Real and Personal Property," 14 Seton Hall Law Journal Review (1984) 485; May,
"Antitrust in the Formative Era: Political and Economic Theory in

Constitutional and Antitrust Analysis," 50 Ohio State Law Journal (1989) 257; Mensch, "The History of Mainstream Legal Thought," in D. Kairys (ed.), The Politics Of Law (2nd ed., 1990); Mensch, "Freedom of Contract as Ideology," 33 Stanford Law Review (1981) 752; Mensch, "The Colonial Origins of Liberal Property Rights," 31 Buffalo Law Review (1982) 635; Minda, "The Common Law, Labor and Antitrust," 11 Industrial Relations Law Journal (1989) 461; Nerkin, "A New Deal for the Protection of 14th Amendment Rights: Challenging the Doctrinal Bases of the Civil Rights Cases and State Action Theory," 1 Harvard Civil Rights — Civil Liberties Law Review (1977) 297; Nockleby, "Tortious Interference with Contractual Relations in the Nineteenth Century: The Transformation of Property, Contract and Tort," 93 Harv. L. Rev. (1980) 1510; Olsen, "The Family and the Market: A Study of Ideology and Legal Reform," 96 Harv. L. Rev. (1983) 1497; Olsen, "The Sex of Law," supra note 5; Peller, "In Defense of Federal Habeas Corpus Relitigation," 16 Harv. L. Rev. (1982) 579; Peritz, "The "Rule of Reason" in Antitrust: Property Logic in Restraint of Competition," 40 Hastings Law Review (1989) 285; Rogers, "The Right of Publicity: Resurgence of Legal Formalism and Judicial Disregard of Policy Issues," 16 Beverly Hills Bar Association Journal (1982) 65; Siegel, "Understanding the Lochner Era: Lessons from the Controversy Over Railroad and Utility Rate Regulation," 70 Virginia Law Review (1984) 187, 250 - 59, 262; Simon, "The Invention and Reinvention of Welfare Rights," 44 MLR (1984) 1; Singer, supra note 17; Steinfeld, "Property and Suffrage in the Early American Republic," 41 Stanford Law Review (1989) 335; Stone, "The Postwar Paradigm in American Labor Law," 90 Yale Law Journal (1981) 1509; Sugarman & Rubin, "Towards A New History of Law and Material Society in England, 1750-1914," in G. Rubin & D. Sugarman (eds.), Law, Economy and Society: Essays in the History of English Law 1750-1914 (1984); Tarullo, "Law and Politics in Twentieth Century Tariff History," 34 UCLA Law Review (1986) 285; Vandevelde, "The New Property of the 19th Century," 29 Buffalo Law Review (1980) 325.

26. *See* Kennedy, "Freedom and Constraint in Adjudication: A Critical Phenomenology," 36 *Journal of Legal Education* (1986) 518; Kelman, "Interpretive Construction in the Criminal Law," 33 *Stanford Law Review* (1981) 591.

27. *See* J. Piaget, *supra* note 23, at 130-31.
28. *See* J. Piaget, *The Moral Reasoning of the Child* (Gabain, trans. 1965).
29. *Ibid.,* at 84-108.
30. *Ibid.*
31. C. Levi-Strauss, *supra* note 10.
32. *Ibid.,* at 48.
33. *Ibid.,* at 67-68.
34. *Ibid.,* at 68.
35. *Ibid.*
36. *Ibid.,* at 123.
37. *See* Kennedy, *supra* note 11; Kennedy, *supra* note 12.
38. *See* Balkin, *supra* note 4.

A LEFT PHENOMENOLOGICAL ALTERNATIVE
TO THE HART/KELSEN THEORY
OF LEGAL INTERPRETATION[1*]

This paper has three parts. The first presents a summary of some elements common to the theories of legal interpretation of HLA Hart and Hans Kelsen. The second summarizes the left phenomenological alternative to legal positivism, as developed by one tendency within critical legal studies (CLS). The third attempts to clarify the alternative through a response to one of the many misreadings of the CLS position that are current in the positivist and post-positivist mainstream of Unitedstatesean academic legal philosophy.

I.

This part concerns the following idea common to Hart's and Kelsen's canonical brief writings on legal interpretation.[2] We imagine the norm that is to be interpreted as an area or space that has two parts. In Hart, there is a "core of certainty" and a "penumbra of doubt," also called a "fringe of vagueness" and an "area of open texture."[3] In Kelsen, there is a "frame, encompassing various possibilities for application."[4] Within the Hartian core, interpretation is "determinate." In the penumbra, it is a matter of discretion, or balancing of conflicting considerations, or judicial legislation, or law making. Outside the Kelsenian frame, the norm is determinate, but within the frame there are alternative interpretations between which the judge must choose, exercising discretion, making law or balancing interests, and interpretation is not determinate.

For Kelsen and Hart, determinacy of a given norm, seen as a unit, is a matter of degree. For Kelsen, constitutional norms defining the proper exercise of legislative power are relatively indeterminate as to what statutes the legislature should adopt, while statutes are relatively more determinate of the content of judicial decisions purporting to apply them. Likewise, for Hart norms can have larger or smaller penumbras, although even standards (e.g., "fair rate") have core meanings.

For positivists, it seems to me, it should be important that for both Hart and Kelsen, the existence of an area of indeterminacy is inevitable for every single norm, and that neither of them provides a clear account of just why this should be true. Moreover, in each case, the use of spatial imagery is a major obstacle to understanding what they mean.[5] But nothing in the discussion that follows seems to me to turn on how we interpret them with respect to this question.

It is likewise striking that both authors seem to use the word determinate in a confusing way. Sometimes, it means only that we can predict with great certainty what the interpreter will do with the problem at hand.[6] At other times, it means that the operation is "cognitive," in the sense that we understand it to be a judgment about a meaning, understood to be something that is independent of the observer, and with respect to which we believe there is a "truth of the matter," even if interpreters are likely to disagree about what that truth is.[7] Again, this will not be an issue in what follows.

What will be important for the analysis that follows is that, for cases in the area of certainty, they speak as though the cognition of a correct meaning for the core or frame, or the highly predictable choice of interpretation, were automatic and effortless, supposing good faith. Kelsen seems completely unself-conscious in assuming that a question is or is not "within the frame." It is a matter of "cognition."[8] Hart is more nuanced in his description of indeterminacy. For him, it is just that "uncertainties" "may break out in particular concrete cases;" cases of unclarity "are continually thrown up by nature or human invention."[9] But a given case just *is*, nonetheless, always located in one metaphorical space or the other.

Perhaps for this reason, each author is sometimes characterized as a "formalist." When they are affirming that, in a particular situation, there is only one right answer to the interpretive question, they read as literalists, however insistent they may be on the discretionary nature of questions located in the penumbra or the frame. It is clear, nonetheless, that each author sees himself as a determined enemy of the mode of legal reasoning that was called formalism in their time, namely conceptual jurisprudence.

Conceptual jurisprudence accepts that there will be situations in which there is more than one valid norm (section of the code or binding precedent) that, *taken in isolation,* is arguably applicable to the facts, and that the different norms will give different outcomes for the case. Conceptual jurists (and their critics, e. g., Gény in *Méthode d'interprétation et sources en droit privé positif*[10]) have also tended to believe that there are situations that are "new" in the specific sense that no valid legal norm was specifically intended to determine them one way or another.

Their method requires the judge to deal both with conflicts and gaps as follows: he is to presuppose the coherence of "the system" as a whole, and then to ask which of the conflicting norms, or what new norm, made applicable to the case, "fits" best with closely related norms. If this is not clear, he moves to the more abstract norms, explicit or implicit in "the system," from which the particular norms are understood to derive (Savigny[11]). Again, he will choose a norm or devise a new norm, but do so without exercising discretion, balancing, or "making law" in the sense of legislation.

From the point of view of H/K, the operation of "construction," through which a conceptual jurist deals with the conflict or gap, is discretionary and "legislative." They consider conceptual jurisprudence to overestimate the determinacy of the legal order, whether we are dealing with norms in isolation or with "the system" taken as a whole. A major virtue of positivism, as they understand it, is to acknowledge or even highlight the judicial lawmaking that conceptualism obfuscates.

Along with literalism and conceptual jurisprudence, a third method of interpretation of legal norms that is current in the Western legal domain is policy analysis, or the method of balancing or proportionality. Here, the interpreter understands himself to have a choice between norms or between formulations of the norm, a choice that is resolved by appeal to the conflicting considerations that he understands to underlie the norm system as a whole.

There are many variants of the method of policy analysis. What is balanced might be conflicting rights, powers, principles, or instrumental goals supposedly of common interest, along with administrative interests (e.g., in certainty *vs.* equitable flexibility), and system architecture interests (e.g., in subsidiarity, or the separation of powers). Or all of the above.[12]

Hart refers approvingly to balancing of this kind as the appropriate method for the penumbra or area of open texture.[13] Kelsen merely points out that it is not a solution to the problem of discretion because it "does not supply the objective standard according to which competing interests can be compared with one another."[14]

For CLS, the important point is that the anti-formalism of H/ K *presupposes* the schema according to which every case is located *either* in the area of determinacy *or* in the penumbra or frame. For our purposes, what counts is not that policy analysis is frequently required and appropriate, but that they provide no account of how the situation gets framed as one located in the penumbra or frame, so that there is no determinate right answer available.

In other words, before the policy analysis begins, whatever its content, the interpreter explicitly or implicitly frames the situation as one in which there is a conflict or a gap that exempts him from the elementary duty to apply a clear norm when the facts clearly fit within its definitions. H/K ressemble the conceptual jurists and the inventors of interest balancing in that they do not theorize this initial framing.

II.

This part offers an account, first, of the process by which interpreters constitute legal situations in either of two ways: either as ones in which all that is required is application of a norm, or as ones in which, because we are in the penumbra or within the Kelsenian frame, or there is a conflict or a gap, something more than mere application of a norm is required (the "something more" being choice among eligible interpretations based on legislative discretion, coherence analysis, teleological analysis, policy analysis or whatever). Second, it offers an account of the role of "ideology" in the process of framing, and then deciding, issues implicating significant "stakes." Third, it applies this conception to the question of how to understand the role of ideology in legal change and legal stability.[15]

A.

In the Hart/Kelsen framework, shared by conceptual jurisprudence and policy analysis, there is no room for the activity that I would place at the center of a phenomenology of cores, frames, gaps and conflicts, a phenomenology that can account for determinacy and indeterminacy. This is the activity of legal "work" understood as the transformation of an initial apprehension (Husserl[16]) of what the legal materials making up the system require, by an actor who is pursuing a goal or a vision of what they *should* require. (The conception of work here is inspired by Marx's *Economic and Philosophical Manuscripts of 1844-1845*.[17])

Legal work, as I am using the term, whether aimed at cores or frames or at penumbras or conflicts or gaps, is undertaken "strategically." The worker aims to transform an initial apprehension of what the system of norms requires, given the facts, so that a new apprehension of the system, as it applies to the case, will correspond to the extra-juristic preferences of the interpretive worker.

Legal work occurs after the initial apprehension of facts and norm, and after "unself-conscious rule application." The interpreter "grasps" (a *gestalt* process, as in Kohler's *Gestalt Psychology*[18]) the situation as a whole as one in which a norm governs and the question is whether particular facts within the situation trigger its application so as to produce a sanction. Someone has died, and the court is asking, first, whether the defendant killed a person, and, second, whether the killing was a legal murder, and that "depends on the facts." Often, once the facts are found, no one will even advert to the possibility of legal work directed at the interpretation of the norm that defines and punishes murder. The facts will be understood to establish guilt or innocence "of their own accord," as the norm "applies itself" seemingly without any agency of the interpreter.

It is familiar that the facts come into legal being through the work of investigators, so that the facts presented depend on the work strategies and levels of effort of prosecutors and parties. It is also familiar that the advocates and the judge, and, at a more abstract level, the jurist, sometimes work to transform the initial apprehension of which norm governs and what it requires. In Chapters I and II of this book, I described, in perhaps excessive detail, the various practices they deploy. Together the practices enable "strategic behavior in interpretation."

These are three types of strategic behavior in interpretation:

First, trying to find legal arguments that will produce the effect of legal necessity for an outcome—that is, for a rule-applied-to-the-given-facts—different from the outcome that initially appeared self-evidently required, as, for example, by making it appear that there is necessarily an exception to the rule that apparently covers the case, or that the "true meaning" of the rule is different than it at first appeared.

Second, trying to make what looked like a self-evidently discretionary judicial decision (one in the penumbra or within the frame) appear to be one in which there is, after all and counter-intuitively, a particular outcome—a rule-as-applied-to-the-facts—that is required by the materials (*i. e.* the case falls within the core; there are no alternatives within the frame).

Third, trying to displace an initially self-evidently legally required outcome with a perception of the situation as one in which the judge is obliged to choose between legally permissible alternative (*i. e.* moving an interpretation from the core to the penumbra or into a frame permitting judicial discretion).

In all these cases, the interpreter works to create or to undo determinacy, rather than simply registering or experiencing it as a given of the situation.

Work presupposes a medium, something that the worker "fashions." In this case, the medium is that body of legal materials that are considered relevant in establishing the meaning of the norm as applicable to the facts. This will certainly include the dictionary, with its definitions, and the legal dictionary with its quite different ones, and doctrinal commentary, and the full body of valid legal norms, perhaps more abstract rights and principles, perhaps legislative debates, perhaps case law. From our point of view, the question is not what count, officially, as "sources," but what elements are sought out and deployed in fact in the work of advocacy or justification.

The worker works using the legal materials to convince an audience of some kind (and himself as well) that an initial apprehension (his or that of another) of determinacy or indeterminacy was wrong. But there is nothing that guarantees that this enterprise will succeed. Work is neither cognition of binding law nor discretion in devising law according to "legislative preference." It is between these two. The legal materials constrain legal work, but in the way a medium constrains any other worker. It constrains only against an effort to make the materials mean one thing or another.

To say that the interpretation of the rule was determinate is only to say that at the end of the work process the interpreter was unable to accomplish the strategically desired re-interpretation of the initially self-evident meaning of the norm as applied to the facts. In other words, critical legal studies, as I understand it, accepts fully the positivist idea that law is sometimes determinate and sometimes indeterminate. CLS rejects both the idea of global indeterminacy and the idea that there is always a correct interpretation, however obscure or difficult to arrive at. But it also rejects the idea that determinacy and indeterminacy are "qualities" or "attributes" inherent in the norm, independently of the work of the interpreter.

Strategic success against initially self-evident determinacy (or self-evident indeterminacy) is a function of time, strategy, skill, and of the "intrinsic" or essential or "objective" or "real" attributes of the rule that one is trying to change, as these appear in the context of the facts presented.

The "ontological" question is whether it is appropriate to regard the determinacy of the rule as applied to the facts, meaning its insuperably binding or "valid" quality at the end of the period allowed for working on it, as its own attribute, something inherent to it. The alternative is that the determinate or indeterminate quality of the rule cannot be understood otherwise than as an "effect," the "effect of necessity" or "effect of determinacy," produced contingently by the interaction of the interpreter's time, strategy and skill with an *unknowable* "being in itself" or "essential" nature of the rule in the given factual context.

The legal worker performs the classic phenomenological reduction or "bracketing" [epoche] (Husserl)[19] of the question of whether the resistance of the rule to reinterpretation is a result of what it "really" is or merely an effect of time, strategy and skill. The worker proceeds by trying to change things, without a pre-commitment one way or another to an ontology of the norm. For the strategic interpreter nothing turns on deciding on the essence. The left phenomenological position within CLS adopts this attitude as well.

B.

Stakes determine how much work to do. Max Weber's distinction between material and ideal stakes is useful here.[20] The litigants may be materially motivated, and the judge too, but judges (and jurists) are obviously often conscious of only ideal stakes. They choose a work strategy because they understand their enterprise as having to do with "justice," understood as non-identical with law application. They also understand the duty to achieve justice as "subordinate" to law. But this duty can be operative only after law is established. The conventional definition of the judicial (or juristic) role doesn't say anything about legal work, because the standard (positivist) model recognizes only cognition and discretion, and makes no place for work.

Those who understand interpretation as either cognitive or discretionary are likely to regard work designed to achieve a particular change in the self-evident meaning of a norm, in a direction that is determined strategically, that is, extra-juristically, as illegitimate. I think the illegitimacy argument is incorrect.

First, most people agree that judges are supposed to work at interpretation, and have to decide how to orient their work. Indeed, most jurists would regard it as a violation of the duties of the judicial role for the judge simply to act on whatever meaning of the norm was initially self-evident, once it had been pointed out that there was another possibility. The reason for this is that the judge knows that work may change the initial appearance. He cannot take it as "true" merely because it is initially legally self-evident.

Faced with the obligation to work in one direction or another, judges (and jurists) often orient their work to the goal of making their extra-juristic or legislative intuition of justice-in-rule-choice into the reality of judicial decision. These are the "activists," in Unitedstatesean parlance. In contemporary legal consciousness, judges working in this way are open to the charge that they are doing this work "ideologically."

In contemporary legal discourse, an ideology is a "universalization project" (Habermas[21]), meaning the assertion of a controversial conception of justice, alleged by some to be mere rationalization of partisan interests, but defended by its adepts as serving the interests of all—*as well as* the interests alleged by its opponents to be merely partial (Mannheim[22]).

The pursuit of an avowedly ideological juristic agenda is problematic for judge or jurist, because even if we readily acknowledge that judges are obliged by their role to work to make positive law correspond to justice, it is a premise of the liberal democratic theory of the separation of powers that ideology is *not for the judiciary (or for the jurist)*, but rather for the democratically elected legislature.

Judges often respond to the dilemma by claiming to work, and attempting to work, non-ideologically—bracketing their legislative preferences in deciding in which direction they will try to move frames or cores. But when they do this, they have to contend with the fact that their audience, and they themselves, understand different outcomes to respond, in many cases with high stakes, to different ideologies.

Two very common judicial (and juristic) postures, in the presence of this dilemma, are "bipolarity" and "difference splitting." In the first, the judge establishes, for himself and others, that he is an ideological "neutral" because he unpredictably alternates between the alternatives defined by conflicting ideologies. In the second, the judge establishes his neutrality by being a "centrist," devising a solution that gives something to each side, but gives neither side all that it demands. These are bad faith solutions, in Sartre's sense in *Being and Nothingness*,[23] because they avoid role conflict through denial (in Freud[24] and Anna Freud's[25] sense).

The position of the "activist" judge, who consciously or unconsciously pursues his own ideological commitments (rather than claiming neutrality because he is a wild card or a centrist), seems to me more ethically plausible. The judge knows that work may make the rule approach his legislative preference, but may not. Suppose he is committed to applying the rule if he cannot destabilize it using accepted, conventional judicial techniques -- that is by research into the legal materials that will lead to their reinterpretation according to accepted canons of legal reasoning.

Then why shouldn't he direct his work, time, strategy and skill, to finding the argument that will make law correspond to his conception of justice? It seems plain, to me, that he would be acting illegitimately precisely if he failed to attempt this, in other words if he failed to make the attempt to rework positive law to make it correspond to his idea of justice. The judicial (and the juristic) role requires fidelity to "law" in the complex sense that combines a positive and an ideal element.

This position, which legitimates juristic work intended to inflect the law in the judge's (or jurist's) preferred ideological direction, is, of course, "anarchist" (or at least "pluralist") from the "Jacobin" point of view that locates legal legitimacy solely in the will of the people. Moreover, it faces a problem of infinite regress in deciding whether the judge has in fact destabilized the norm using only what I just described as "conventional judicial techniques." But the alternatives that condemn judicial work *a priori* are worse, because they are incoherent, given our societal understanding of the requirements of the judicial role.

C.

If we recognize that judges can and do work to change cores or frames (whether or not we regard this work as legitimate), then a basic Hart/Kelsen notion is undermined. This is what Kelsen calls the "dynamic conception,"[26] in which the movement of norm creation is from the abstract to the particular or concrete. In Hart, it is the notion that adjudication "fills in" the penumbra, as well expressed by MacCormick in the following quotation.

> The thesis that even the best drawn laws or lines leave some penumbra of doubt, and this calls for an exercise of a partly political discretion to settle the doubt, is not particularly new, it is but the common currency of modem legal positivism...
>
> A crucial point, though, is that one ought not to miss or under-estimate the significance of line-drawing or *determinatio* as already discussed. The law really does and really can settle issues of priority between principles by fixing rules, and even when problems of interpreting rules arise, these focus on more narrowly defined points than if the matter were still at large as one of pure principle. Fixing rules can be done either by legislation or by precedent; most commonly, in a modern system, by the two in combination. It is one of the gifts of law to civilization that it can subject practical questions to more narrowly focused forms of argument than those which are available to unrestricted practical reason.[27]

If strategically directed work in interpretation can disrupt initial apprehensions of cores or frames, then this statement is much too optimistic about the "gifts of law to civilization." In my extended treatment of this topic,[28] I suggested that "small" questions can have very large ideological stakes. Second, I suggested, contrary to MacCormick, that the same arguments of principle recur at each level of abstraction, so that settling issues "further down" in the pyramid will involve arguments no less controversial than those that apply at the top. This is the argument from the phenomenon of "nesting" discussed in Chapter 2 of this book.[29]

For our purposes here, there is a quite different point: even after an interpretation is settled, work can destabilize it. This means that work can "inflect" or "shift" cores and frames. There is now a "from the bottom up" dynamic that counteracts to one extent or another Hart and Kelsen's top down, abstract to concrete, dynamic. Rather than MacCormick's progressively narrower focus for issues of controversy, the worker can hope to split open cores or dissolve them.

So work does more than fill the frame or the penumbra dynamically with strategically determined norm choices. Ideology inflects work, which inflects frames and cores, which in turn provide, in the coherence view, means to further destabilizations of other cores and frames.

In this view, the body of valid law, that is law that is regarded by legal workers in their initial encounter with the materials as core or frames, is well understood, first, as an historical work product of lawyers, jurists and judges who have pursued (some of the time; consciously or unconsciously) conflicting ideological projects (which may be centrist, in the above sense), and, second, as always but unpredictably subject to destabilization by future ideologically oriented work strategies.

III.

In order to understand the above position--possibly the dominant position within critical legal studies since about 1985, and, today, the only remaining explicitly argued CLS position--it may be useful to contrast it with a typical misreading of CLS from within

the mainstream of Anglo-American legal philosophy, in this case
by my friend Brian Bix:

> [I]n particular, CLS theorists argued for the radical in-
> determinacy of law: the argument that legal materials do not
> determine the outcome of particular cases. CLS theorists
> generally accepted that the outcomes of most cases were *pre-*
> *dictable*; but this was, they claimed, not because of the de-
> terminacy of the law, but rather because judges had known
> or predictable biases. The legal materials, on their own, were
> said to be indeterminate, because language was indetermi-
> nate, or because legal rules tended to include contradictory
> principles which allowed judges to justify whatever result
> they chose (Kelman 1987). The CLS critiques have gener-
> ally been held to be overstated (Solum 1987); though there
> may well be cases for which the legal materials do not give a
> clear result, or at least not a result on which everyone could
> immediately agree, this negates neither the easiness of the
> vast majority of possible disputes nor the possibility of right
> answers even for the harder cases.[30]

1. The left-phenomenological CLS tendency (probably the
dominant tendency) proposed that legal materials do or do not
determine the outcomes of cases only in interaction with the
argumentative strategies of jurists pursuing objectives with limited
time and resources. The materials are one part of the determination, but only in combination with interpretive activity that is not
cognitive but rather consciously or unconsciously strategic. It is not
and never was the position of this tendency within CLS that "legal
materials do not determine the outcome of particular cases," but
rather that their influence is mediated, and that their "intrinsic" or
"essential" determinacy or indeterminacy is unknowable.

The legal materials are "indeterminate" only in the sense
that sometimes it is possible to destabilize initial apprehensions
through legal work—"intrinsically" or "essentially" they are neither

determinate nor indeterminate. True, we often initially apprehend them as determining the outcome of a particular case or, on the contrary, as not determining the outcome (because the case falls in the penumbra or within the frame). In one type of apparent determinacy, we predict a result *because we anticipate that no work will be done to destabilize the initial apprehension*. And it will often be possible to predict that no such work will be done, because the extant ideological projects empowered through the judiciary are likely in agreement with the initial apprehension, or in agreement that the outcome is not worth destablilizing work. We might anticipate that it would be otherwise if actors with radical or other outlying ideological projects more commonly worked as judges or as influential jurists.

In a second type of case, the legal materials appear determinate when, after legal work to the point of exhausting the time and resources available, the prognosticator finds himself or herself unable to destabilize the initial apprehension that there is an applicable norm, and that that norm decides the case for one party or another. S/he will predict a result *because s/he anticipates that work done to destabilize the initial apprehension will fail*. The prediction of an outcome of the interaction between the facts as presented, interpretive work, and the unknowable "essence" of the materials is based on the belief that the decision-maker will be unable to come up with a good argument for an alternative outcome. Again, the centrist ideologies shared by judges and jurists in capitalist countries are an important factor in this kind of prediction.

CLS writers have worked from the beginning, and continually, to figure out how rules, particularly of property and contract, that seem likely to resist even the most sustained effort at transformation through interpretation, given the moderate left or moderate right ideological preferences shared by virtually all judges in all capitalist countries, have massive and unjust impacts on oppressed groups. This is the CLS contribution to the sociology of law and left wing law and economics.

2. The notion that the indeterminacy of language explains the way in which law is indeterminate has had some influence in CLS,

particularly on the early work of Unger,[31] and on writers like Boyle,[32] who purported to speak for CLS as a whole. From the beginning, a more influential current argued that rules vary in "formal realizability," or "administrability," so that the simple linguistic critique is often trivial, as are all other arguments for "global" indeterminacy.[33]

Bix's attribution to CLS of a notion that "legal rules [tend] to contain conflicting principles" is puzzling. The CLS claim was, a la Dworkin,[34] that principles, policies and rights, and indeed worldviews, are all part of the commonly deployed sources of law, but, contra Dworkin, that they are in ineradicable conflict, within each of us as well as between us. Their conflictual presence is reflected in the more concrete "valid legal norms of the system," which CLS, following legal realism, understands to be, *always*, complex compromises of those conflicts.[35] Because the rules are compromises, rather than a coherent working out of one or another over-arching principle, they are much more open to destabilizations of various kinds than coherentist writers acknowledge.

3. The "biases" of judges are relevant because they orient legal work by judges (and other jurists) to transform initial apprehensions of what the materials require in the particular direction suggested by the jurist's material or ideal interests (loosely, the jurist's ideology). Whether the jurist will succeed in the work of making the materials conform to his ideological or material extra-juristic strategic motive is never knowable in advance (though, as with any uncertain future event, we can make odds). Jurists constantly accept interpretations according to which the positive law is contrary to their view as to what it ought to be.

Moreover, "biases" or ideology do not determine jurists' work strategies any more conclusively than the system of legal norms determines outcomes. Ideologies are indeterminate in just the way that the legal order is. There is a hermeneutic circle at work here, in which the indeterminacies of each level get resolved by appeal to a deeper level with its own indeterminacies, and so on, back to the starting point, in which legal ideas influence ideology as well as vice versa.[36]

4. The CLS critiques have been held to be overstated (or to indicate incompetence or insanity) within a mainstream that has misunderstood them more or less in the manner of Brian Bix in the above passage. They also are quite often misinterpreted, not as above, but as claiming "determination in the final instance" by the base, or as a vulgar Marxist claim that the judges are the "executive committee of the ruling class," and proceed case by case to further "the interests of capital." The misreadings derive in part from the more or less complete ignorance both of phenomenology and of critical social theory among mainstream Unitedstatesean legal theorists, in part from the limited resources that mainstream legal philosophers devote to marginal currents (Bix is exceptional in his familiarity with CLS writing), and in part to the normal investment of mainstreams in reproducing the marginality of the margins.

5. Everyone knows that "there are cases for which the legal materials do not give a clear result." And that there are cases in which the legal materials do not give a result "on which everyone could immediately agree." But it is quite another matter to assert that there is a burden on the CLS type of critique to "negate" "the easiness of the vast majority of possible disputes."[37] This quantitative claim has an important place in the positivist, or at least the Hartian scheme. It serves to reassure us that the recognition of judicial discretion in the penumbra poses no threat to the liberal value of the rule of law. According to Hart, the "rule-sceptic" is welcome "as long as he does not forget that it is at the fringe that he is welcome; and does not blind us to the fact that what makes possible these striking developments by courts of the most fundamental rules is, in great measure, the prestige gathered by courts from their unquestionably rule-governed operations over the vast central areas of law."[38]

The CLS claim is that the question of what proportion of actual or imaginable disputes have determinate outcomes, given the legal materials, has to be asked taking into account the possibility that legal work will destabilize the initial apprehension of what the materials require. Determinacy is a function of the words of valid norms, and of the content of other sources, *and also* of their interaction with the resources and strategies of whoever has the power to do legal interpretation, *and also* of the "thingness" of the materials and the facts as presented. Once we take this into account, statements about the "vast majority of disputes" or "vast central areas of law" are simply meaningless.[39]

6. That results are not determinate in some cases, according to Bix, does not "negate the... possibility of right answers even for the harder cases." The only intelligible meaning of a "right answer" in a case, hard or easy, given the phenomenology above, is that having worked with the time and resources available and according to a chosen strategy, the interpreter can't find an alternative to some particular apprehension of what rule applies and what it requires when applied. In other words, after performing the phenomenological reduction, the "right answer" is the one that is produced by an argument having the "effect of necessity." As to whether there is a right answer in the sense of one available to cognition, CLS takes the position of Kant as to the "thing in itself."

Notes

1. The first draft of this paper was prepared for a conference on Problemas Contemporaneos de la Filosofia del Derecho at the UNAM in Mexico City under the title, "A Left Phenomenological Critique of the Hart/Kelsen Theory of Legal Interpretation" and published under that title in the proceedings of the conference, Cáceres et al., eds., *Problemas Contemporáneos de la Filosofía del Derecho* (Mexico City, 2005). That version was translated into Dutch and published as "Een linkse fenomenologische kritiek op de rechtsvindingstheorie van Hart en Kelsen," in 3 *Nederlands tijdschrift voor Rechtsfilosofie & Rechtstheorie* 242 (2004). This is a substantially revised version. Thanks to Imer Flores and Brian Bix for helpful comments. Errors are mine alone.

2. HLA Hart, *The Concept of Law* (Oxford, 1961)[hereafter Hart]; Hans Kelsen, Introduction to the Problems of Legal Theory (B. Paulson & S. Paulson, trans. Oxford, 1992 [1934])[hereafter Kelsen].

3. Hart, e.g., 119-20, 123-26, 128, 131, 135, 143, 150.

4. Kelsen, 77-81.

5. See for useful discussions Letizia Gianformaggio & Stanley Paulson, *Cognition and Interpretation of Law* (Torino, 1995).

6. Hart, for example: "The plain case, where the general terms seem to need no interpretation and where the recognition of instances seems unproblematic or 'automatic,' are only the familiar ones, constantly recurring in similar contexts, where there is general agreement in judgments as to the applicability of the classifying terms." At 123. For a useful discussion, see Brian Bix, *Law, Language and Legal Determinacy* (New York, 1993).

7. Hart speaks of "plain, indisputable examples of what does, or does not, satisfy [general standards]." The "general agreement" part has disappeared here. P. 128. Kelsen, when discussing the bringing in of extra-juristic considerations at the moment of law creation within the frame, speaks of "room for cognitive activity *beyond discovering the frame within which the act of application is to be confined.*" At 83.

8. Kelsen, see n. 6 above.

9. Hart, at 123, 132.

10. Francois Geny, *Méthode d'interprétation et sources en droit privé positif: essai critique*, 2nd ed. (Paris, 1919).

11. Friedrich von Savigny, *System of the Modern Roman Law* (W. Holloway, trans., Madras, 1867).

12. See generally, Duncan Kennedy, "From the Will Theory to the Principle of Private Autonomy: Lon Fuller's Consideration and Form," 100 *Colum. L. Rev.* 94 (2000); Duncan Kennedy, "The Disenchantment of Logically Formal Legal Rationality, or Max Weber's Sociology in the Genealogy of the Contemporary Mode of Western Legal Thought," 55 *Hastings L. J.* 1031 (2004); Duncan Kennedy & Marie-Claire Belleau, "La place de René Demogue dans la généalogie de la pensée juridique contemporaine," *Revue interdisciplinaire d'études juridiques*, vol. 56, p. 163 (2006).

13. Hart, e.g., 126-30.

14. Kelsen 82.

15. This section is largely a summary of the approach proposed in "Freedom and Constraint in Adjudication," which is Chapter 1 in this volume, and in Duncan Kennedy, *A Critique of Adjudication [fin de siecle]* (Cambridge, Mass., 1997), Parts 1 & 3.

16. Edmund Husserl, "The Natural Attitude and its Exclusion" (1913) in Edmund Husserl, *The Essential Husserl: Basic Writings in Transcendental Phenomenology* (Donn Welton, ed., 1999) 60

17. Karl Marx, "Economic and Philosophical Manuscripts" in *Writings of the Young Marx on Philosophy and Society* (L. Easton & K. Guddat, eds. & trans. New York, 1967 [1844]).

18. Wolfgang Kohler, *Gestalt Psychology: An Introduction to New Concepts in Modern Psychology* (New York, 1947).

19. Husserl, op cit. p. 65.

20. H.H. Gerth & C. Wright Mills, "Introduction" to *From Max Weber: Essays in Sociology* 61-65 (New York, 1946).

21. Jurgen Habermas, 1 *The Theory of Communicative Action: Reason and the Rationalization of Society* 16-19 (T. McCarthy, trans. Boston, 1984)

22. Karl Mannheim, *Ideology and Utopia: An Introduction to the Sociology of Knowledge* (New York, 1936).

23. Jean-Paul Sartre, *Being and Nothingness: An Essay on Phenomenological Ontology* (H. Barnes, trans. New York, 1965.

24. Sigmund Freud, *Sexuality and the Psychology of Love* (New York, 1963).

25. Anna Freud, *The Ego and the Mechanisms of Defense* (C. Baines, trans. London, 1937).

26. Kelsen, s. 43, p. 91

27. Neil MacCormick, "Reconstruction after Deconstruction: A Response to CLS," 10 *Oxford J. Leg. Stud.* 539, 553-54 (1990).

28. *A Critique of Adjudication [fin de siecle], supra,* 172-173.

29. See Chapter II of this book. "A Semiotics of Legal Argument," 42 Syracuse L. Rev. 75 (1991). The extended version reprinted in this book is available in 3 *Collected Courses of the Academy of European Law,*

Book 2, 309-365 (Kluwer Academic Publishers, Netherlands 1994)

30. Brian Bix, "Law as an Autonomous Discipline," in *The Oxford Handbook of Legal Studies* 983 (Peter Cane and Mark Tushnet, eds. New York: Oxford Univ. Presss, 2003). The Kelman reference is to Mark Kelman, *A Guide to Critical Legal Studies* (Cambridge, Mass.: Harvard Univ. Press, 1987). The Solum reference is to Lawrence Solum, "On the Indeterminacy Crisis: Critiquing Critical Dogma," 54 *U. Chi. L. Rev.* 462 (1987).

31. Roberto Unger, *Knowledge and Politics* 88 (New York, 1977).

32. James Boyle, "The Politics of Reason: Critical Legal Theory and Local Social Thought," 133 *U. Pa. L. Rev.* 685, 710-11 (1985).

33. Duncan Kennedy, "Legal Formality," 2 *J. Leg. Stud.* 351 (1973); Duncan Kennedy, "Form and Substance in Private Law Adjudication," 89 *Harv. L. Rev.* 1685 (1976).

34. Ronald Dworkin, "The Model of Rules," in *Taking Rights Seriously* (Cambridge, Mass., 1977).

35. "From the Will Theory," *supra*; "The Disenchantment," *supra*.

36. *A Critique of Adjudication, supra,* 187-91.

37. Bix, *supra.*

38. Hart, at 150. See also p. 149, 141-21, 132.

39. Chapter I of this volume, p.   *A Critique of Adjudication, supra,* 172.

THOUGHTS ON COHERENCE, SOCIAL VALUES AND NATIONAL TRADITION IN PRIVATE LAW[1*]

My aim in this brief essay is to reflect, very much from an outsider's point of view, on three concepts or notions that seem to recur in the discourse of my European colleagues (and friends) who are working on the Europeanization of private law. The first is the notion of "the coherence of private law," as in the sentence: "The Commission's directives threaten to destroy the coherence of private law." The second is the notion of "the social values of European law," as in the sentence: "Harmonization should reflect the social values of European law." The third is the notion of "the particularity of national legal traditions," as in the sentence: "Harmonization should be respectful of the particularity of national legal traditions."

I don't mean to suggest that these sentences are everywhere or that every scholar or even most scholars working in this area would agree with them, not at all. But coherence, social values and national tradition come up quite often. I have the impression that not using, or refusing to use, one or another of these concepts defines one's position negatively but sometimes clearly. As an American participant/observer in this discussion over the last few years, I have come to recognize in myself a moment of puzzlement. The three notions are virtually never explicated fully. They are each quite complex. The relationship between them is not clear.

So, for example, it has occurred to me to ask: "Do those who think that what is important in harmonizing is the fate of social values reject the idea of coherence?" "Do they care about national traditions otherwise than as the vehicle for preserving social values?" And so forth. "Does reference to preserving the coherence of private law mark one as a political conservative or as a methodological conservative—or both, or neither—and do we expect conservatives to reject social values in private law?"

If I were a European, I imagine I would have a much better idea than I do about how to answer these questions, because I would have a better idea of what is meant by coherence, social values and national tradition in European private law discourse. Not being a European, I thought I might contribute to the discussion by summarizing and elaborating, for what it's worth, some of my own work, not likely to be at all familiar in Europe, on each of these notions as it appears in the American context.

I. COHERENCE

The notion of coherence does not play a central role in the everyday discourse of private law in the US. Three explanations: (1) US law is so thoroughly lacking in coherence that no one would think it useful either to criticize it or to reform it with coherence in mind. (2) The notion of the coherence of private law was central to Classical Legal Thought (CLT) in the US, and was critiqued in a devastating way by the sociological jurists and legal realists, so that we Americans are "beyond" it, unlike Europeans who may have invented the critiques but lost touch with them after the Second World War. (3) Coherence is the obsession of private law legal theorists in the US, from Fried and Barnett to Macaulay and Macneil to Posner, and also of Dworkin, but goes under other names (e.g., "fit"), or is unnamed (and jurists operating below the abstract level of legal theory have little interest, for reason one or reason two above).

But before beginning the discussion of coherence, I have to confess something well described as "profound puzzlement" about what Europeans are referring to when they speak of "private law." Sometimes it seems they are speaking of the sections of Continental civil codes that cover the law of obligations; sometimes that they mean to include family law; and sometimes that they mean to include along with the law of obligations the various statutory regimes covering labor law, consumer law, landlord tenant law, the law regulating land use beyond the law of private nuisance, and so forth. And where does the regulation of sexuality and reproduction through good faith, good morals and *ordre publique* clauses in the civil codes fit into the discussion of private law? What about commercial law?

The question of definition is obviously important for a discussion of coherence. For example, Wieacker, in his famous discussion of social law, states emphatically that the social law of labor, tenancy, environment, etc, has "destroyed the coherence of private law."[2] He seems to think, though it is not clear, that the code law of obligations was and perhaps still is coherent, but that the subtraction from it of these domains of statutory regulation poses two juristic problems. The first is that social law is not itself coherent, but rather ad hoc. The second, only implicit, is that we cannot regard the whole of his broad private law category as coherent unless we have coherent criteria to explain what parts have remained in the "individualist" codified core and which have been selected out.

Then there is the fact that the new Dutch civil code apparently reverses the secular tendency to preserve coherence by segregation, and re-includes the regulatory domains, and that the Mussolini era Italian civil code seems to combine the elements without an effort of conceptual integration. What do these points about arrangement indicate? Certainly not, as far as I can tell, that the sense of incoherence has disappeared in the new synthesis for which Wieacker (plaintively) called.

A jurist adopting an external point of view, i.e., engaged in trying to characterize a private law regime as an observer, might describe a legal order as coherent or not coherent in various ways. A jurist adopting the internal point of view will always or at least generally have chosen, explicitly or more likely implicitly, one or another of these before s/he sets out to try to state a rule or body of rules "correctly."

Total coherence (everyone knows it's impossible). The external observer, or the jurist before s/he begins internally oriented work, might think, though I don't think any do in fact think, that the system of private law was coherent in a very strong sense. All the rules of the system, s/he might think, follow (in some sense, tightly or loosely, etc) from a set of principles that are either consistent with one another, or apportioned among parts of the rule system through meta-principles that are consistent with one another.

These principles might be capable of resolving any new situation arising within their respective domains. For example, s/he might think that labor law is fully governed by a consistent set of social principles, whereas contract law is governed by a consistent set of individualist principles, and that the boundary between contract law and labor law is clear (for example, because labor law covers all transactions involving labor power as a commodity). Obviously no one claims that the private law of any country is coherent in this maximal sense.

Coherence at the level of principle. The observer might conclude that the system contains, as the basis for legal interpretation, a set of principles that are either consistent with one another or apportioned to parts of the system according to a coherent set of meta-principles. In this version, it is understood that many concrete rules of the system may be inconsistent with the principles that should govern them and that there may be conflicts, and that gaps may appear as new cases arise.

The observer might conclude that the principles and meta-principles enable jurists to "operate" the system, in the sense of coming up with solutions to problems posed by past errors, and solutions for some, but not necessarily all, conflicts and gaps. These solutions, in this model, follow, for the jurist doing particular interpretations, either as a matter of meaning from the principles correctly understood, or from correct teleological reasoning from the principles understood as goals of the legal order. In this model, there can be deep and long standing disagreement about the correct application of the principles, and even about what exactly the principles are, without putting into question the idea that the system is coherent, albeit in this more modest mode.

The private law regimes of the different European states could be coherent in this sense, and there could be a coherent "European private law" in this sense, even if the lower level rules of the different states were very different. The differences would simply be instances of disagreement about how to perform the interpretive task given the shared larger principles.

A jurist who regarded the system as coherent in this manner could treat the interpretive task as to carry out the "logic of the system" by choosing the solution to the question at hand that seemed to him or her to be dictated by the applicable principles within the given area of law. Indeed, this approach might seem to be compelled by the very idea that the jurist has adopted the internal point of view, given that the coherent set of principles is part of the legal order, and solutions seem to follow from the elucidation of their meaning or purpose. On second thought, this is not as obviously correct as it at first appears.

The jurist could decide to adopt a particular solution, or a whole set of solutions, that differ from those dictated by the principles and meta-principles, on the ground that there exists a meta-meta-principle, say, of adaptation of the law to changing social realities, or of preservation of supra-legally defined individual rights. In this case, the jurist's solution will make the private law regime less internally coherent that it was before, unless the jurist redoes the whole thing at one blow.

Putting the "logic of the system" into effect would then be reduced to one of the goals of legal interpretation, to be "traded off" against other goals. At the extreme, the jurist could regard the putting into effect of system logic as irrelevant to the juristic role, understanding himself or herself, say, as obliged to decide cases "on their individual merits," or to choose the "best moral solution," or to put a "higher law" into effect, even when any of these conflicted with system logic.

Speaking of the US system from the internal point of view, I think the argument that there is a meta-meta-rule that the jurist's job is to enact the system's logic is wrong. I prefer the view of Cardozo: that the jurist is sometimes acting morally and professionally correctly when s/he interprets according to morality or justice or policy against the solution s/he believes required by coherence.[3] But I also find the whole discussion of limited interest, because most jurists, myself included, long since stopped perceiving or presupposing that private law as a whole (i.e., including social law and family law as well as the law of obligations) is endowed with coherent substantive principles for fields along with meta-principles for apportioning cases among fields.

The reasons for the change in perception or presupposition about private law are probably many and complex, but we certainly share across the Atlantic a common narrative, already alluded to, in which the rise of "the social" is the main culprit or hero, depending. I have already mentioned Wieacker's version, in which the core of private law remains coherent, while the social subtractions from the core destroy the coherence of the whole field, because they are themselves internally ad hoc rather than principled, and (perhaps) we lack principles for deciding when to subtract and when not to.

American critics have tended to reject the Wieacker formulation. First, the core of private law has never been coherent, and, second, the social subtractions, while not coherent, are far from ad hoc. In this view, the law of obligations even in its purest late 19th century civil law or common law forms and most technical domains (e.g., offer and acceptance, conditions) was structured internally by the conflict of individualist and altruist strategies.[4] Moreover, fields like labor law and landlord/tenant represented compromises of these same factors, situationally determined by the balance of forces, but in no way piecemeal or chaotic.[5]

Family law was the same. Although supposedly based, in the Savignian scheme, on an anti-individualist principle of intra-family fusion, the field was in fact internally contradictory in a way strictly analogous to the law of obligations and social law.[6] (This way of describing the structure of private law is sometimes called "nesting," or "chiasmus" or the "fractile" quality.[7]) Finally, the divisions between the law of obligations, social law and family law now appear arbitrary rather than commonsensical or practical.

Coherence as "the effect of necessity."[8] That conflict and contradiction at the level of principle seem (to me) to be everywhere in private law does not mean that jurists experience no differences in doctrinal structure, from field to field, or between sub-fields within a domain. My approach has been to try to substitute for the notion of coherence, understood as consistency or non-contradiction at the level of principle, the notion that a jurist who has an "agenda," or a "how-I-want-to-come-out," will experience legal fields as differing in the degree to which they produce "the effect of necessity." The effect of necessity is the sense, with respect to an actual or hypothetical case, that the legal materials dictate a result.

The legal materials in the US and European systems include enacted norms (both very concrete ones and more abstract principles), decided cases, and doctrinal authorities' views about what the norms are or ought to be. They also include canonical projects of rationalization of particular decisions and whole fields, whether produced by judges or by academics. When the jurist perceives the field to be governed by elaborate legislation, which has given rise to many judicial decisions that include sustained reasoning about what norms govern beyond the legislative ones, and there is dense academic commentary that is in agreement about what the norms are, what they mean, and that they fit together harmoniously, we might describe the field as "impacted."

As cases arise, we expect that jurists will find "straightforward" solutions, and lawyers will advise litigation only when the stakes are high enough to merit taking a chance on a counter-intuitive result, or the client has an eccentric motive for refusing to settle. Other fields may look quite different. For instance, in a "contradictory field" the observer notes that both the enacted principles and the principles adduced by judges and scholars are conflicting, and that there are many cases, with facts close together, seeming to derive from each principle. New cases will commonly pose the interesting question of which conflicting principle will be judged to govern, which analogies will be deemed persuasive, and so forth.

Another possibility is that the field will initially present itself as "unrationalized," with few decisions, little relevant legislation, an undeveloped scholarly literature, and few attempts at rationalization either in opinions or in doctrine. Here, as in the contradictory field, the effect of necessity will be weak or absent when new cases present themselves. This list of types is obviously not exhaustive.

This approach is phenomenological, in the sense that it asks not whether a given field is "really" or "truly" coherent in the sense of consistently principled, but whether it is experienced as structured so as to compel particular results in many cases. A crucial aspect of this approach is that it can take into account that the jurist's initial perception or cognition of the field is not the end of the story. The reason for this is that the jurist can choose to work on the field, trying to change the way s/he and others perceive it.

The possibility of doing juristic work on the field is obvious for the lawyer advocating for a client, but no less real for the judge or the academic. Even in an impacted field, that is, one that presents itself as both coherently and densely regulated, it is always open to the jurist to try to reformulate not just the facts of a particular case but also the relevant norms and their rationales, so that what appeared at first blush the inevitable result is reversed, or at least rendered questionable.

The motives for this activity may vary. One motive is the financial gain of the advocate, another the jurist's search for the "truth of law," and another the urge to make law correspond to an extra-juristic view of what would be the just outcome or the best legal norm in the circumstances. But the motive is irrelevant in the sense that the procedure of legal work to reconfigure the field, thereby modifying the effect of necessity, is legitimate according to the meta-meta-principles of Western legal systems.

At the same time, it is open to the jurist to simply accept the initial apprehension of the field, with whatever effect of necessity it generates in the case in hand, and move on. In other words, work is permitted and perhaps morally required of both the lawyer and the judge or academic, but work time must be allocated, and often it makes sense to accept, say, that the field is so impacted that work to destabilize it is wasted.

Let's suppose the jurist decides to work on the field, for whatever legitimate reason. The work will change the field, making it, for example, impacted in a different way with a different result in the case at hand, or making it less impacted or more impacted, more or less contradictory, more or less rationalized. The jurist who sets out to work on the field can adopt various points of view with respect to these effects.

These vary from field-type to field-type, but the most interesting for our purposes is the case of the impacted field that the jurist wishes to reconfigure so as to produce a different result in a case, or different results across a broad range of cases. For example, the project of promoting objective liability in worker accidents or in tort in general in the late 19th century context of a highly developed law of negligence. Or the modern US project of "tort reform" by reducing liability for defective products by changing multiple sub-rules of the pro-plaintiff regime that emerged between 1945 and 1980.

The jurist might reject any such agenda outright, adopting the position that coherence is the only legitimate goal for his or her work. S/he might regard it as permissible to intervene to shape the field, by describing and re-describing it in order to make it as coherent as possible, but impermissible to have an agenda as to the substantive outcomes that are made more likely by the particular version of coherence produced. Joseph Raz[9] trenchantly critiques this position, arguing that once we recognize that coherence is relative and local, and that the interpreter is dealing with a question that has not been "authoritatively" settled, then s/he should work toward the most morally desirable outcome (with morality understood to be the sum of legitimate motives in interpretation).

The substantive commitment to deciding "morally" is distinct from that of preserving the coherence of the field, because more morality might require less coherence. In other words, the jurist might end up making the conflicts between principles and the inconsistency of results more rather than less salient. As Raz recognizes, this doesn't make coherence "irrelevant," since there may be good reasons to give it weight in deciding what the morally correct solution to a given problem might be. It merely reduces it to the status of a policy to be balanced with others.

Raz seems to me to reify the distinction between the "authoritative" and the "morally correct," and so to miss the significance of juristic work on each of the poles. He also slights what has traditionally been the most important of the motives for giving coherence weight. This is the idea that impacted fields constrain judicial power, both in the sense of judicial discretion in assessing particular cases, and in the sense of judicial legislative power to develop new rules.

In the approach I have been developing here, the reason for this is that it takes more work to destabilize an impacted field than to rationalize a result in a contradictory field or defend a solution in an unrationalized field. In other words, without conceding for a minute that legal fields can be "truly" or "essentially" coherent in a way that constrains the judge, we can eagerly affirm that configurations that are experienced as impacted are more resistant than others, because more work, without a guarantee of success, will be required to fight what at first blush seems the obvious and inevitable outcome.

One of the instrumental reasons Raz points out for giving weight to preserving coherence derives from the interdependence of the elements in a given field and the limited ability that a judge or jurist (as opposed to the idealized legislator) has to re-work a whole field at a single blow. Looking for the ideal rule to cover one aspect of the situation may be counterproductive, given the presence of elements the jurist is at least temporarily powerless to transform. For example, if a system combines a strong commitment to fault with strong compensatory and punitive damage rules, moving to strict liability without reducing the damage measures could produce a less than ideal new balance of externalized and internalized costs allocated to plaintiffs and defendants.

What counts as a legitimate motive for giving weight to coherence depends as well on one's theory of the judicial (or juristic) role. For example, suppose that the judge believes that his or her solution in a given area will be controversial. In this case, s/he may want to maximize the impacted character of the field configuration toward which s/he is working, in order to "make it stick," that is, to make it difficult for subsequent jurists to destabilize it. In other words, coherence can appear as a mere instrument of a particular substantive agenda, rather than as a value in itself. Depending on how one assesses the legitimate role of politics or substance in the judge's professional self-understanding, this might be a legitimate or an illegitimate reason for giving coherence weight.

The devolution, so to speak, of coherence as the supreme legal value is part of the story of the rise of the social, already described. The reduction of coherence to a policy, and possibly to a mere instrument of substantive agendas, fits into the story of the gradual rise of balancing, or proportionality, or "conflicting considerations" as the default method of legal reasoning in Western legal systems. This development permits a reformulation of coherence in a new and much more modest mode.

Coherence as proportionality.[10] This fourth, modest type of coherence is that of a system in which the conflicting principles that animate it are named, there are criteria for acceptable principles, and decision is by the method of proportionality or balancing when the prior methods of textual exegesis and local coherence at the level of principle don't work in solving particular problems. The most important criteria for acceptable principles in systems understood to be coherent in this way are: (a) that they should be enacted, or explicitly adopted in case law, or at least inferable from the body of norms recognized to be valid; (b) that they should be universalizable in the Habermasian[11] if not necessarily in the Kantian sense (so that materially distributive or sectarian religious or politically ideological principles are excluded).

Coherence as proportionality can have normative power. It can, sometimes, guide or influence or even strongly constrain decision. It can generate the "effect of necessity," just as simple exegesis and coherence at the level of principle can, sometimes, do this. It is radically different from coherence at the level of principle because it operates by restricting what can be a principle (the requirements of positivity and of universalizability) and then by prescribing the method of proportionality. The effect of necessity is generated, first, when the jurist (with his agenda, or his "how I want to come out") finds that s/he can't find a plausibly intra-systemic universalizable principle to support that desired outcome and has to accept another one.

Second, the process of adjudication over time generates precedents that have to be interpreted as instances of balancing or weighing acceptable principles, understood as "real," that is, as existing in the normative plane like objects with gravitational fields in the physical world. A precedent establishes relative weights for a given case. A new case is "a fortiori," *vis-à-vis* a precedent, if the new case seems to involve the same principles to be balanced, and the principle held to dominate in the first case seems even more dominant in the new one.

The jurist who decides to work to destabilize the effect of necessity generated by the materials, in order to support a specific outcome or to reconfigure some subset of outcomes, has to re-order the principles, restate and reinterpret the facts of cases, and perhaps introduce new principles. Once again, as with coherence at the level of principle, there is no guarantee of success, but also no way of establishing ex ante that the work will fail.

The conflicting principles that have to be balanced in a weakly coherent system of this type can include all the different kinds of principles that all agree animate modern legal orders. Rights as principles are understood in this mode to be chronically (though not necessarily always) in conflict. This sense has been growing steadily for fifty years as more and more constitutions combine social rights and classic individual rights, or attach a social clause to the classic rights, as in the frequent case of declaring the social function of private property. The "constitutionalization of private law" has turned out to be closely connected to the rise of proportionality as legal method.

But there can be conflicting utilitarian principles (efficiency by internalizing costs versus efficiency by maximizing freedom of action) and conflicting moral principles (pacta sunt servanda sed rebus sic stantibus). General clauses in codes embed this possibility. Principles of different types can be balanced against one another, as in rights vs. efficiency, and rights can also be balanced against powers—national security vs. civil liberties, etc.

Proportionality can be the method for adjudicating among powers as well as among rights, including conflicts of separated governmental powers (judiciary vs. legislature vs. executive) or among the elements of a federation or a transnational formation like the European Union, or between domestic and international instances. The principles can also be at the level of system maintenance. For example, a right can be balanced against the need for certainty or flexibility.

The great reassuring virtue of coherence at the level of principle, the reason why one would want to preserve the impacted character of fields and work to make contradictory or unrationalized fields impacted whenever possible, is that the more of it there is, the less likely it is, in theory, that the interpreter will confront a gap or conflict without guidance. Coherence will seem less important where the legal culture takes it for granted that most questions can be resolved "exegetically," meaning by appeal to the meaning of norms taken one by one. In the same vein, proportionality will seem less important in a legal culture where it is assumed that coherence at the level of principle will almost always work. As faith in exegesis weakens, coherence takes over. As faith in coherence weakens, the interpreter is forced to resort to the method of proportionality.

Proportionality is thus historically a "counsel of despair." A key factor in its emergence has been the work of internal critique by jurists pursuing their particular agendas, each "clearing the ground" as a preliminary to their preferred reconstruction of legal reason in the wake of the rise of the social. The cumulative impact of these efforts has been not reconstruction, but the progressive revelation of just how much "abuse of deduction" or "social conceptualism" has been necessary to preserve the idea that Western legal systems secure the separation of powers.

It is therefore quite nonsensical to say things like: "I have a problem with proportionality, which is that it is a weak form of rationality and lacks certainty and is manipulable," if the speaker means that we should therefore stay with exegesis and some form of principled coherence. No one proposes proportionality until they believe that stronger modes are simply unavailable in the circumstances, typically because in the area in question the conflict of principles (or purposes) seems inescapable.

When we understand the legal order in terms of the balancing of conflicting principles (broadly understood as above), we still experience fields as differently configured. They are still impacted, contradictory, unrationalized, and so forth. As in the case of coherence at the level of principle, we can ask whether it is legitimate for the jurist to work to produce an outcome s/he thinks is just, at the expense of the impacted or coherent character of the field, but now in the sense of a field where the principles are a defined set and there are many cases that seem to establish relative weights consistently. Here, as with coherence at the level of principles, the jurist works to generate the effect of necessity for the desired outcome. But this can involve de-rationalizing as well as rationalizing the field.

We can ask whether there is a meta-meta-rule of the system that says that, if you can't figure out a way to make a convincing proportionality argument for your solution, you have to abandon it. Or whether, on the contrary, there is a meta-meta-rule that allows rejecting the balance of principles as previously established in case law, in favor of a solution that will represent social justice, or justice in the particular case, or adaptation to social change, or supra-legal rights, or whatever.

The weakness of proportionality from my point of view is not that it is unprincipled, but that it is excessively principled. The universalization requirement for principles, along with the odd (neo-Kantian) imagery in which principles are treated as normative vectors analogous to physical forces, impose restrictions on the judge that I think he should be ready to discard when they conflict with his intuition of justice in a sufficiently important case. The Habermasian ambitions of proportionality seem to me to be in denial as to the truth of our ethical experience of undecidability. Aren't they pre-modern? Pre-Kiekegaard, pre-Nietzsche, pre-Weber, pre-Schmitt?[12]

II. SOCIAL VALUES

"The social," as I am using the term here, was originally a critique of the "individualism" of the rules of classical private law. Social values were required to modify the individualist rules, because those rules ignored "interdependence." The social, of course, could be right wing or left wing or centrist. But in whatever form, its advocates saw individualist law as having a very strong internal logic, based on the will theory, a sharp public/private distinction, the notion of "spheres" of absolute property and contract rights, and induction/deduction as the preferred methodology.

As the social people saw it, this conceptual structure led directly to a set of dysfunctional positive law regimes. It led to a labor law regime in which unions could not bind their members *in invitum*, to fault as the basis of industrial accident law, to a regime of no liability of landlords for defective premises or for the public health externalities of slum properties, to *caveat emptor* across the board in consumer law, and to the under-regulation of securities markets. A social regime was designed to make actors liable for the consequences of their actions in "an interdependent world," taking into account inequality of bargaining power and the dangers of "downward spirals," with "adaptation to new social conditions" and "the public interest" as the guiding normative ideas.[13]

I don't think this is exactly what European private lawyers mean today by social values, although in their discourse there is quite frequent allusion to this earlier analysis, and the specific reforms brought about by the social current remain as the starting point for modern advocacy of social values. In place of the analysis in terms of interdependence, adaptation to new social conditions and the public interest, today's rhetoric seems to be that of "solidarity" and "weak parties."

Particular weak parties are defined in relation to particular strong parties, as: workers in relation to employers, women in relation to men, consumers in relation to professional sellers, the poor in relation to the middle class and the rich, illegal immigrants in relation to legal immigrants and citizens, the chronically unemployed vis-à-vis the employed, children vis-à-vis adults, the mentally ill vis-à-vis the "normal," the physically disabled vis-à-vis the abled, and so forth. Solidarity means a private law regime that takes the weakness of weak parties into account, and tries to compensate for it, in defining their legal relations with strong parties.

The social ideology initially asserted a new reality of interdependence, and the consequent danger to the social whole of individualist law, with the public interest as the criterion for deciding on reforms. The current framing in terms of solidarity with weak parties is quite different. It is much more explicitly "distributive," in the sense of advocating private law rules that require strong parties to make concessions to weak parties, for the good of the weak parties. The argument that oppressive social conditions are a threat to the "normal" middle class citizen, because they breed crime or disease or industrial warfare or terrorism, for example, is still present, but it has lost primacy to a more straightforwardly ethical argument. The imperative of solidarity seems to be based on a notion of human rights or social rights or human dignity or "love of the other" or common membership in the national community.

The easy formula of solidarity is to reject discrimination against weak parties, meaning differences in formal legal treatment. A second easy meaning is to work against their marginalization, against societal blindness to their situation, against the failure to pay attention to their suffering and allocate resources to alleviate it. In the law of obligations, these are not the focus. The focus is on restricting freedom of contract between strong and weak and on broadening the scope of tort liability of the strong to the weak. In social law, the focus is on the coverage of social safety nets and on their cost, and on limiting freedom to opt out of protection. In the law of sex, reproduction and the family, the issues involve traditionalist claims of cultural pluralism against the liberalized law of the dominant culture, the claims of Western traditionalism against those same liberalizers, the claims of cultural feminists against libertarian or queer feminists, and the like.

When the rules at stake regulate markets through contract and tort law, it puzzles me that Europeans interested in social values in private law don't seem to have answers to criticisms of the social that are standard and dangerously powerful in the United States. The first of these is that restrictions of freedom of contract, where there is no price control, lead the strong party to pass on the cost of protection to the beneficiaries, forcing them to take something they would not voluntarily contract for and forcing some of them out of the market.

The second criticism is even more serious. It is that social protections in general, when they do indeed benefit the class of weak parties, operate by cross-subsidies that are prima facie unjustifiable. The more traditional version of this argument is that strong protection for workers in formal employment is at the expense of the weakest part of the labor force. The weakest sector suffers higher unemployment as a result of high costs, and when employed in the informal sector gets no protection at all. High levels of social benefits in general are feasible only so long as they exclude the people at the bottom of the pyramid, who may be illegal immigrants or just the poor, and, in the American case, predominantly African American populations of formerly industrial urban centers.

The more recent version is the inverse. Protections against risk in consumer law or accident law supposedly operate as a cross-subsidy from the more responsible or competent part of the weak group to the less responsible and competent. For example, products liability and welfare require the responsible and competent members of the lower middle class and working classes to subsidize the irresponsible, opportunistic and venal at their level or below them. Social law seems to demand solidarity among weak parties, at least as the parties conceive themselves, rather than between the weak and the strong. (The dilemma is mockingly referred to in Italian as the problem of "*socialismo in una sola classe.*")

The third problem is that social law is implicated in identity formation: by rewarding irresponsibility, opportunism and venality, it supposedly promotes these as character traits. This has been argued for a generation for the case of welfare dependency, but the legal representatives of strong market actors have transferred the argument to consumer protection, tenant protection, and so forth. Regulating the contracts of the strong with the weak destroys their incentive to look after themselves while offering them opportunities to cheat the protective system at the expense of their more responsible co-contractors.

My own view is that these arguments are sometimes valid but much more often spurious and even dishonest. But it seems necessary to have a way to analyze the pursuit of social values in private law, whether understood narrowly as the law of obligations or widely to include social law. This mode of analysis has to deal with the economic arguments on their own terms, rather than simply denouncing the Commission as neo-liberal when it declares that freedom of contract is the rule and protection an exception that bears the burden of proving its efficiency.[14]

In short, the phrase social values is not self-explanatory when we are speaking of private law rules of contract and tort. The frank assessment of distributive and identity formation effects seems necessary.[15] Is this just the paranoia of an American left that has seen the social program lose its political base to the argument that, rather than promote justice between the strong and the weak, or even between the middle class and the working class, it shifts resources around within the bottom half of the income distribution, leaving everyone discontented for one reason or another?

When we move from the private or social law of markets to the law of reproduction, sex and the family, the notion of social values acquires a whole new set of ambiguities. Familial relations were a constant though often implicit reference in the development of the social program for the market. The law of interdependence was supposed to recognize that the larger social whole organized through the market had many of the characteristics of the family. The duties of the patriarchal household head, which the 19th century had little by little restricted to the nuclear blood family and then rendered unenforceable as merely "moral," were, in effect, to be re-imposed on employers and owners in the public interest broadly conceived.

But the reference to the family was ambiguous. On the one hand, the family was the locus of duties of solidarity; on the other it was the locus of relations of authority based on gender and paternity. The social program for the family could be progressive, involving enforcing the high moral duties that Classical Legal Thought had recognized but rendered unenforceable (e.g., no domestic abuse, child support). It could look to the bad societal consequences of denial of rights to illegitimate children, denial of a right to divorce, denial of rights to mistresses, denial of a right to abortion, denial of rights to prostitutes, outlawing of homosexuals, and produce a highly progressive reform agenda.

But it could also go in the opposite direction, supporting the reinforcement of paternal power, the accentuation of male/female role differentiation (separate spheres) and the policing of sexual behavior, in the name of the social bond and the welfare of society as a whole. In the post Second World War period, just as the social in the market became more and more associated with a left rather than a traditionalist (e.g., social Catholic or fascist) agenda, so the social in the law of reproduction, sex and family became more and more associated with authority and tradition, whether Catholic, Greek Orthodox, Islamic or fundamentalist Protestant.

The conservative discourse of opposition to abortion, for example, or to parenthood for same sex couples, is very explicitly one of solidarity, with the fetus or the child. In short, the social in the law of reproduction, sex and the family has the opposite political valence from the one it has in the law of the market. Meanwhile, progressives have more and more adopted liberal egalitarian, or autonomy-based, as opposed to social rationales for reform. Their discourse has strong undertones of Classical Legal Thought, deploying tropes that are considered reactionary in the law of the market.[16]

As in the law of the market, the issues involve the distributive consequences of different legal regimes, and these are possibly even more complex than those in the market domain.[17] For example, the rules governing the rights of mistresses and prostitutes affect the welfare of wives. Issues of identity are prominent, both as the basis for positions about legal rules and as stakes that will be affected by what legal rules are in force.

The border between the market domain and that of sex, procreation and the family is unstable: the wife who guarantees her husband's debt to a commercial bank is inside the law of obligations, but brings the ambiguities of the meaning of the social with her from family law, along with the distributive complexities of consumer protection law. The good faith, good morals and public order clauses in continental civil codes, as they apply to sex, reproduction and family relations, make any attempt at a clear boundary problematic.

None of this means that the social is merely ad hoc. Rather it means that it is a contested concept, as is liberal individualism. This becomes even clearer when we ask its relation to the full domain of policies and interests that are involved in disputes about private law in a transnational context. For example, among the questions that the social does not answer unequivocally, in situations of at least formal national independence and at least formal internal democracy, is how power should be distributed among law making institutions.

In what we might call the horizontal dimension, courts, legislatures, administrative agencies, academics and powerful litigants (multinational corporations, NGOs) all struggle to control the making of private law. There is a discourse as to the proper distribution of power among these institutions that may sometimes be merely instrumentalized by those with social or liberal individualist agendas. But sometimes what the actors care about is not the underlying "substantive" issue at stake, but rather the appropriate distribution of power between, say, the judiciary and the executive, seen as a value in itself. The same is true as to the distribution of power over private law between the local, regional, national and European levels, with the issues cross-cutting that of horizontal distribution between courts, legislatures, etc.[18]

Without belaboring the point, all this means that it is not possible, as it once was, to use the opposition between liberal individualism and the social as an overarching orientation to private law. That distinction, moreover, had the purpose and the bad effect of masking the irreducible element of left/right politics, and other forms of politics as well, that inhabit the process of private law making.

But ... it won't work to resolve these complexities by embracing the ideological division between left and right as the "real" explanatory variable and the "real" source of normative orientation. The reason for this is that modern leftism and rightism are no more internally coherent than liberal individualism and the social. The left/right opposition, like the individualist/social opposition, is indispensable when we try to understand our situation as lawmakers and the orientations to action not just of others but of ourselves as well. But neither is adequate if by adequate we mean adequate to warrant confidence in ourselves in the decisionist moment.[19]

III. NATIONAL TRADITION

This section is less developed than the two that precede it, more of a sketch for future inquiry than a developed position. National private law systems, within some set that we single out for analysis, can differ in many ways. They can have different rules governing similar cases. For example, one system might have adopted a regime of liability without fault in products liability whereas another might use negligence. Different systems develop different legal concepts to govern broad areas, as for example the contrast between the English and the Continental systems in that the English reject good faith in contract law while it is central to the German and German influenced systems, or that the Continental systems make the notion of patrimony a key to the law of damages whereas the English do not.

Then there are national differences in juristic method. These can be quite formal, as in differences in the way legal judgments are written and reasoned, or implicit, as in differences in the degree of "formalism" or "policy orientation" characteristic of legal reasoning in general. In the old days, it was common to believe that there were many profound differences between the common law and the civil law. But it was also common to think that the French were more "exegetic" than the Germans. One system might give professors more actual power as authorities than another, whatever the doctrine of "sources" might specify.

At some point, it makes sense to use a stronger word than mere difference to contrast systems. Tradition, or culture, affirms that there is something very "basic" at stake in a particular difference.[20] "Respect for the particularity of national legal traditions" appeals to this sense of serious or profound difference. The notion of tradition or culture is the basis for an argument: when we set out to assess or reform or harmonize a set of systems, there is something to take into account—tradition or culture—other than how "we," the jurists operating trans-nationally, feel about the substantive solutions to legal problems adopted in the systems in question.

It might be an argument for limiting the area to be harmonized, in order to avoid areas where conflict in national rules is great, or of great symbolic importance. It might be an argument for harmonizing slowly rather than rapidly. It might be an argument for harmonizing by "soft law" rather than "hard law." It might also be an argument for harmonizing not by regulatory soft law but by "dialogue" between jurists, professors, judges and others, of different systems.

There is a parallel between the argument for respecting tradition and the argument for respecting the coherence of a system. Each presupposes a possible tension between forward looking, substantive, moral or utilitarian or political considerations, and the valued "isness" of the system in question. We might ask Raz's question about tradition: if there is no "authoritative" rule at stake, or if the jurist (harmonizer) is in the position of the legislator, is there any reason at all for respecting tradition at the expense of "morality" or substantial justice, however we define it? Supposing that we reject, here as in the case of coherence, the position that tradition should simply trump all other considerations, we need to ask in what sense it is "relevant."

As with coherence, the kind of important difference that we might want to call tradition turns out to have quite different possible meanings. We might begin by distinguishing two extreme positions on how to understand the evident differences among national legal systems within some set, which might be the whole world, or a region (South America, the Arab Middle East, Europe) or a federal system with autonomous sub-national private law authorities (the US). The first is organicist and the second "semiotic" (used here to avoid the ambiguity of the word "structuralist").[21]

National traditions might be "organic" in the sense that they are one of the important parts that constitute and are dialectically constituted by the "whole" of a national culture or spirit. Each national whole would be unique, a product both of abstract cultural traits and of the vicissitudes of a specific national history. Within the whole that is the national culture, the legal tradition would also be a whole, that is, an entity with its own peculiar animating spirit and its own history. The elite that produces it might be more or less open, for example, to foreign legal cultures, and to one or another aspect of the surrounding national culture. We understand historical change in organisms of this kind, whether at the national or the legal level, through the images of growth, development, maturity, decay, etc.

It is crucial but difficult to keep distinct the different senses in which we deploy the metaphor of the organism. Using organicist methodology, we treat the civil law, the common law and any other system that interests us as an organism. But it is common to use the adjective "organic" to describe a trait, as when the British harbor the conviction that their tradition is in some sense "more organic" (less rationalist or less mechanical) than the civil law tradition. This mode links to Burkean rather than Savignian organicism, in which implicit, and perhaps rationally ungraspable deep-seated laws of the whole, when the whole is British, are always in danger from well meaning utopian meddling.[22]

This often seems silly to an American. The British seem to believe simultaneously that they decide the case on the facts, that they practice precedential formalism, and that they are actually more policy oriented than the continentals.[23] In any case, respect for national tradition, following Raz, shouldn't mean respect for the elements that seem confused or behind the curve or philistine in the tradition, no matter how organic the traditionalists believe their tradition to be.

The metaphor of the organism is also at the root of functionalism in comparative law, linked as it is to the idea that law "adapts" to "social conditions," so that we expect similar societies to develop roughly similar solutions to similar problems of their type of social order. This form of organicism allows us to identify as worthy of respect in the national tradition (i.e., entitled to weight when we have to decide) the interdependence of the elements of a national solution to a typical dilemma of social order. So the harmonizer must take into account that a partial harmonization may upset a nationally specific balance, say between formalism in offer and acceptance and informalism in quasi-contract. This means that there may be bad spill-over effects, in particular national systems, of the adoption of particular rules that seem on balance clearly better, taken in isolation, than the rules they replace.

It is worth noting that "respect for national tradition" is here close to "preserving the coherence of private law"—in this case, an implicit coherence evident to the eye of the comparativist, rather than the formal coherence of enacted principles. It is also worth noting that this form of comparative law functionalist coherence is the intellectual product of the social current, starting with Lambert.

I don't think we can dispense with this kind of organicist thinking, in spite of the dangers of vagueness, romantic exaggeration and obscurantism (the familiar critique of Savigny's *Volksgeist*). It even seems to me undeniable that there are national differences, for example, in the standard array of available character types (not *the* national character type) within which individuals develop infinite variations. It also seems plain to me that there are unities of this kind that we grasp intuitively, pre-reflectively. When a person fails to grasp pre-reflectively in this way, they come across as incompetent in dealing cross-culturally.[24]

The semiotic view of national particularity rigorously rejects organicist accounts of national difference. We imagine that the national legal elites, across the set that interests us, operate with a common conceptual vocabulary for specifying the terms of a legal rule, and with a common repertoire of potential rule solutions for new problems and arguments pro and con. They come up with different specific rules to govern specific cases, but we should understand these as "parole," in the "langue" of regional legal discourse.

This is a very specific adaptation of the Saussurian distinction. The valid norm, or the proposed valid norm, is like a sentence—a unit of legal speech. Thus a jurisdiction's rule that the contract by correspondence is valid on the mailing of the acceptance is a normative utterance; in the same legal langue, the jurisdiction might have "said" instead that it was valid only on receipt. Or the rule might be that where the offeror revokes after mailing of the acceptance, but before receipt, he is liable only for the reasonable reliance of the offeree (and not for the expectancy).

We explain the choice of one utterance rather than another on offer and acceptance not by a reference to the national culture viewed as a whole, but by a reference to the balance between forces that are represented in every country in the set. For example, we might try to explain a large number of rules by reference to the balance between social and individualist values prevalent in the jurisdiction. The idea is that national traditions, across the geographical space that interests us, don't exist except as accumulated speech. Of course, to the extent that nationals participate in the illusion that they possess national legal traditions, that belief may influence what they choose to "say."

Though this approach is often mechanistic and reductionist (the familiar critique of Levi-Strauss's structuralism), I don't think we can dispense with it any more than we can dispense with organicism. It sometimes seems undeniable that what participants understand to be a highly original, contextually determined (national) discourse appears in a wider view to be no more than the playing of the changes on a rigidly pre-determined set of options.

The notion of legal consciousness,[25] as developed in American critical legal studies, is a kind of compromise of organicist and semiotic approaches, operating (like "coherence as proportionality") as a counsel of despair. In this case, in despair of transcending the opposition of the two methodologies (compare the problem of wave and particle theories of light[26]).

The notion of consciousness is a heuristic: it is a "way of looking" at a legal order; it is a checklist of elements whose identification in a context may make the context more "intelligible." The concept has three dimensions. First, legal actors are acquainted with a vast number of positive rules of law, however established and however problematically or unproblematically "valid." Second, legal actors understand this mass to be organized or structured horizontally, into fields, and vertically according to principles. Fields, as already suggested, can be more or less impacted, contradictory, unrationalized, etc. This is the "structure" of the consciousness.

Third, the dynamic dimension of the consciousness is a langue, which provides a vast legal lexicon and a set of rules of operation through which actors produce proposals as to legal rules, proposals that do or do not get enacted, and "grammatically correct" legal arguments for and against rules (e.g., this rule is good because it promotes security of transaction vs. this rule is good because it permits equitable flexibility).

The first, positive dimension of norms and the second conceptual dimension of horizontal and vertical arrangement are the product of the third, discursive dimension of legal practice. They are parole spoken in the langue. It is crucial to understanding this scheme that there are an infinite number of "grammatically" correct norms, legal arguments and conceptual orderings available to be "spoken" in the legal langue, just as there are an infinite number of possible grammatically correct sentences in an ordinary language. What actually gets "said" (that is, enacted as the norm

or put forward as a legal argument) is, of course, "channeled" by
the pre-existing mass of rules and the conceptual order, as well
as by more complex elements such as Sacco's "cryptotypes"[27] and
Bourdieu's "habitus".[28]

We study the history of a consciousness by the genealogical
method (of Nietzsche[29] and Foucault[30]), looking not for origins,
but for the pre-existing elements that actors combine at moments
of change to produce a new version of the consciousness as positive
order, conceptual arrangement and langue. Again following Foucault, the history of legal consciousnesses in the West is marked
by conceptual and linguistic transformations that go beyond incre-
mental change, and a given consciousness is likely to retain these
in a sedimentary or "layered" pattern, with the new superimposed
on remaining dispersed elements of the old, rather than generating
a new totality.[31] Organic metaphors are perfectly appropriate to describe the processes of change in this kind of quasi-whole.

Consciousnesses in relation to one another. In the modern order of
national legal systems, we can distinguish systems as more or less
open or closed, both internally, *vis-à-vis* the national "society," and
externally, *vis-à-vis* the legal world beyond their national borders.[32]
We can also distinguish systems as more or less integrated with
other systems, in the sense of sharing a larger or smaller quantum of
positive norms, conceptual ordering and langue. External openness
means interaction, but may or may not lead to integration.

In the case of the US, the state jurisdictions, which have (within federal constitutional limits) final say over their private law regimes nonetheless are relatively open to one another and relatively
integrated from the point of view of norms, conceptual arrangement and langue. Up to the First World War, the American private
law system viewed as a whole was relatively open to the British and
Continental systems, and integrated first with the British and then
with the Continental at all levels. After the Second World War, it
turned relatively closed *vis-à-vis* the rest of the world, while remaining relatively integrated. We might ask similar questions, although
I certainly would not dare to answer them, about South America,

the Arab Middle East and Europe, viewed as ensembles of private law sovereigns.

National legal consciousnesses existing in a system of relative openness and integration, as say in the United States, South America, the Arab Middle East and Europe can be seen as sharing a common regional consciousness—can be seen this way, that is, when it seems useful to see them this way. Such a regional consciousness will be in a relation of relative openness or closedness vis-à-vis other systems of comparable scale. A major issue for all the regional systems today is their relation of openness and integration vis-à-vis the United States.

National tradition and social values. Using the notion still in this very loose, merely heuristic way, I would suggest that over the last 150 years, there has been a series of three world scale Western trans-national legal consciousnesses— Classical legal thought, the Social, and contemporary legal consciousness— that have provided conceptual structure and a langue for many national systems worldwide.[33] National systems that received CLT or the Social or the contemporary mode have put them into effect ("spoken them") in different ways. With the advent of the social, for example, they developed different regimes for industrial accidents, regulation of slum housing conditions, and so forth. These are parole, in the sense of utterance in the transnationally developed and nationally received langue. The specific regimes are infinitely varied in detail but fall into a relatively small number of patterns, reproduced in country after country.

Contemporary legal consciousness on a world scale is characterized by, among other things, the perennial unresolved conflict between classical and social approaches to private law, with the odd structure described above, in which the social is progressive in the law of the market and traditionalist in sex, reproduction and family law (with classical individualism the opposite). One way to understand national diversity is to see it as simply diversity of solutions, within a common conceptual structure and with a common langue, reflecting the strength of these tendencies in different countries, on different issues, at different times. In other words, national tradition would be no more than another way to describe the relative strength of classical and social trans-national forces as they have played out in specific contexts.

But this mode of explanation is always incomplete. It explains nothing to say that the choice of a rule was "caused" by the "balance of forces," unless we have an explanation of why the balance was one way rather than another. Such an explanation moves from the trans-national and semiotic to the contextual, at which point we will face once again the choice between organicism and the semiotic as modes of understanding. It is nonetheless worth noting that in Europe today it seems as though every country except Britain claims that one of the things that is distinctive about its national tradition is its highly social character.[34]

The dimension of domination. Within a transnational system like the European, and between trans-national consciousnesses, there will be various kinds of complex relations of hierarchy, power, dominance, hegemony, and so forth.[35] One issue of dominance has to do with the constitution and diffusion of the trans-national consciousness for the region. Jurists in some countries have more input than those in other countries, and some countries are well described as receiving rather than producing developments in the conceptual structure and langue.

Strong countries also influence other countries directly. The modes of influence include forceful imposition of elements of the transnational consciousness (Napoleon, Stalin, legal reform in Kosovo), bargaining (legal reform as a condition of admission to the EU), and prestige. The reception process, however, is always complex. Reception is carried out by local jurists who have interests and orientations, so that there is always an element of "selection," along with the element of imposition. The national systems are so complex and so embedded in the non-legal national culture, and the elements imposed or received are so ambiguous (they are classic floating signifiers), that the reception process is a producer of difference as well as of integration.[36]

The rhetoric of tradition in private law. In this context, appeals to national legal traditions, along with appeals to the European legal tradition, can have many meanings. I mean the next five paragraphs as a provocation rather than as a scientific observation. Quite possibly every assertion is false. I would say, in my defense, only that, as a left over 1960s person, I miss in the discourse of my progressive European colleagues the kind of reductive analysis I try here.

My impression is that when the Germans or French appeal to the particularity of their national traditions in private law, they understand themselves to be speaking from a strong sense that each is really and truly different from other European countries. But they also speak as hegemonic legal powers, with spheres of influence. They have a long-term investment in their dominance not just in the North, East and South of Europe but also internationally (the ex-empire for France; the countries of the BGB for Germany). As competitive hegemonic powers they are somewhat conscious of one another and influence one another, but neither is much influenced by the countries within its sphere, let alone by countries in the sphere of the other.

When they appeal to the European legal tradition, it seems sometimes that they mean to constitute an entity under their joint influence that can countervail the influence of US dominated global contemporary legal consciousness. For conservatives, the tradition in private law turns out to mean the high-class legal science of the will theory and Classical Legal Thought, against the putative incoherence and totalitarian tendency of the social, and against American sloppiness. For progressives, it turns out to mean the social, often defined against the putative hyper-individualism of American law and culture.

National legal tradition seems to have a different function for the British and Scandinavians. They seem to understand themselves as very different from their neighbors, but minoritarian, with no chance of becoming dominant anywhere in Europe. The British are proudly organicist, not to say primitive, and the

Scandinavians are the opposite, claiming to be at once the most social in the law of the market and the most liberal in family law.

For each, one strategy is to resist integration, with tradition being an appeal for relative closure, or a negotiating strategy to minimize how much they will have to give up. Another strategy is to play up the idea of a European legal tradition in order to constitute a transnational space within which, working as cosmopolitans, they have a chance of exercising more influence than would be possible in a world of dispersed national systems with strong German and French blocs.

I find it harder to characterize the way the categories of national and European legal tradition work in the legal consciousnesses of countries within spheres of influence, or at the eastern limits where rejoining an imagined European tradition seems more important than any difference internal to Europe, or even than the differences between European and US legal consciousness. The Italians and Dutch require a category (or two) of their own. But I think these uncertainties on my part are symptoms of the strength of relations of domination in Europe, which orient observation as they differentially authorize Europeans to speak with authority and self-confidence.

IV. CONCLUSION

I don't think the kind of elaboration I've attempted here of coherence, social values and national tradition is likely to be directly helpful in developing positions about the Europeanization or harmonization of private law. Although I've tried to phrase them in a vocabulary that is transnational, my points remain very much rooted in the American experience, and in American approaches to private law theory. The conclusions I reach with respect to each notion are bland: there are many possible interpretations; it doesn't make sense to use the notions without specifying which version one means; the extreme and therefore clear versions are not helpful; the plausible ones are full of ambiguities; each notion is sometimes useful in understanding private law and in thinking about it normatively, provided it is treated as an invitation to further work and study. But none of the notions will help us avoid a decisionist moment.

I do think that it emerges that the three notions are quite closely related: the vicissitudes of coherence are linked to the rise of an ideology of social values, and the particularity of national traditions often refers to supposedly distinct ways of incorporating and developing social values. Above all, I hope I've managed to extend an invitation to European colleagues to push beyond these outsider observations toward a common theoretical base for the discussion of Europeanization, a discussion that seems to be perhaps the most interesting underway in private law anywhere.

Notes

1. *Thanks to Daniela Caruso, Maria-Rosaria Marella and Martijn Hesselink. Errors are mine alone.

2. Franz Wieacker, *A History of Private Law (with Special Reference to Germany)*, trans. Tony Weir (New York, 1995) pp. 431-41.

3. Benjamin Cardozo, *The Nature of the Judicial Process* (New Haven, 1957) p. 98.

4. Duncan Kennedy, "The Political Stakes in "Merely Technical" Issues of Contract Law," 1 *European Review of Private Law* 7 (2001). Duncan Kennedy, "Form and Substance in Private Law Adjudication," 89 *Harv. L. Rev.* 1685 (1976).

5. See Duncan Kennedy, "The Political Significance of the Structure of the Law School Curriculum," 14 *Seton Hall L. Rev.* 1 (1983). Karl Klare, "The Judicial Deradicalization of the Wagner Act and the Origins of Modern Legal Consciousness: 1937- 1941," 62 *Minnesota L. Rev.* 265 (1978).

6. Frances Olsen, "The Family and the Market: A Study of Ideology and Social Reform," 96 *Harvard Law" Review* 1497 (1983).

7. See Chapter 2 of this book. D. Kennedy, "A Semiotics of Legal Argument," 42 *Syracuse L. Rev.* 75 (1991): reprinted with European Introduction: Four Objections and bibliographies in 3 *Collected Courses of the Academy of European Law*, Book 2, pp. 309—365 (Kluwer Academic Publishers: Netherlands 1994). Jack Balkin, "Nested Oppositions," 99 *Yale L. Rev.* 1669 (1990).

8. See Chapter 1 of this book. See generally, Duncan Kennedy, *A Critique of Adjudication [fin de siècle]* (Cambridge, Mass., 1997), Duncan Kennedy. "Freedom & Constraint in Adjudication: A Critical Phenomenology," 36 *J. Leg. Ed.* p. 518 (1986).

9. 8 Joseph Raz, "The Relevance of Coherence," 72 *B.U. Law Review* 273 (1992).

10. See generally Duncan Kennedy, "The Disenchantment of Logically Formal Legal Rationality or Max Weber's Sociology in the Genealogy of Modern Legal Consciousness," 55 *Hastings L.J.* 1031 (2004); Duncan Kennedy, "From the Will Theory to the Principle of Private Autonomy: Lon Fuller's Consideration and Form," 100 *Colum. L. Rev.*

94 (2000); Robert Alexy, *A Theory of Constitutional Rights*, trans. J. Rivers (Oxford. 2002); David Beatty, *The Ultimate Rule of Law* (New York, 2004); Francois Ost & M. van de Kerchove, *De la pyramide au réseau? Pour one théorie dialectique du droit* (Brussels, 2002).

11. Jurgen Habermas, *The Theory of Communicative Action* (Cambridge, 1986-1989) Vol. 1.

12. Duncan Kennedy, "A Semiotics of Critique," 22 *Cardozo L. Rev.*1147 (2001).

13. See Duncan Kennedy, "Three Globalizations of Law and Legal Thought in *The New Law and Economic Development. A Critical Appraisal*, David Trubek and Alvaro Santos, eds., (Cambridge, 2006)[Earlier version: "Two Globalizations of Law and Legal Thought: 1850-1968," 36 *Suffolk Univ. L. Rev.* 631 (2003).] Duncan Kennedy, "From the Will Theory," n. 9 above. Duncan Kennedy, "The Disenchantment," n. 9 above. Duncan Kennedy & Marie.-Claire Belleau, "Francois Geny aux Etats-Unis," in *François Gény, Mythe et Realites 1899-1999: Centenaire de Methode d'Interpretation et Sources en Droit Prive Positif, Essai Critique* (Claude Thomasset, Jacques Vanderlinden & Philippe Jestaz, eds., Montreal, 2000).

14. See, for attempts to do this kind of defense of the social in private law, Duncan Kennedy, "Distributive and Paternalist Motives in Contract and Tort Law," 41 *Maryland L. Rev.* 563 (1982); Duncan Kennedy, "The Effect of the Warranty of Habitability on Low Income Housing: "Milking" and Class Violence," 15 *Fla. St. L. Rev.* 485 (1987); Duncan Kennedy, "The Legal Economics of Low Income Housing Markets in Light of Informality Analysis," 4 *Journal of Law and Society* 71(2002). See also the articles by other authors pursuing a similar agenda on the Housing page of my website, www.duncankennedy.net.

15. See generally. Duncan Kennedy, "The Stakes of Law or Hale and Foucault!" 15 *Legal Studies Forum* 327 (1991).

16. See generally, "Three Globalizations," note 12 above.

17. Duncan Kennedy, "Sexual Abuse, Sexy Dressing and the Eroticization of Domination," 26 *New England Law Review* 1309 (1992).

18. See Fernanda Nicola, "Constitutional Asymmetry and the Transformation of European Federalism: The Europeanization of Private Law" (unpublished paper available from the author).

19. Kennedy (1997) n 7 above; Kennedy (2001) n 11 above; Kennedy (2004) n 9 above.

20. See Danieala Caruso, "The Missing View of the Cathedral: The Private Law Paradigm of European Legal Integration," 3 *European Law Journal* no. 3, p. 19 (1997).

21. See generally, Kennedy, n 11 above.

22. See Robert Gordon, "Law and Disorder," 64 *Indiana L.J.* 247 (1989).

23. This puzzle is illustrated by Basil Markesinis, "A Matter of Style," 110 *L.Q.R.* 607 (1994).

24. See generally Herbert Marcuse, *Reason and Revolution. Hegel and the Rise of Social Theory* (Boston, 1968).

25. See Duncan Kennedy, *The Rise and Fall of Classical Legal Thought* (Washington , D.C., 2006); Duncan Kennedy, "Toward an Historical Understanding of Legal Consciousness: The Case of Classical Legal Thought in America: 1850-1940,". in Steven Spitzer (eds), 3 *Research in Law & Soc.* (1980); Duncan Kennedy, "The Structure of Blackstone's Commentaries," 28 *Buffalo Law Review* 205 (1979); Kennedy, (2000) n 9 above: Kennedy (2003) n 14 above.

26. Paul Feyerabend, *Against Method* (London, 1988).

27. Rodolfo Sacco, "Legal Formants: A Dynamic Approach to Comparative Law," 39 *Amer. J. Comp. L.* 1343 (1991).

28. Pierre Bourdieu, *Outline of a Theory of Practice*, R. Nice, trans. (Cambridge, England, 1977).

29. Friedrich Nietzsche, *The Genealogy of Morals: A Polemic*, R. Hurley trans. (New York, 1924).

30. Michel Foucault, "Nietzsche, Genealogy, History", in D.F. Bouchard (ed), *Language,
Counter-Memory, Practice: Selected Essays and Interviews*, D.F. Bouchard & S. Simon trans, (New York, 1977).

31. Michel Foucault. *The History of Sexuality, Volume III*, Robert Hurley, trans. (New York, 1990).

32. Maurizio Lupoi, *Sistemi giuridici comparati: Traccia di un corso* (Naples, 2001).

33. See generally Kennedy, Three Globalizations, n. 12 above.

34. See *id.* for a similar point in the global context.

35. Diego López Medina, *Teoría impura del derecho: La transfor-*

mación de la cultura jurídica latinoamericana (Bogotá, 2004).
36. Cf. Gunther Teubner, "Legal Irritants: Good Faith in British Law or How Unifying Law Ends Up in New Divergencies," 61 *Modern Law Review* 11 (1998).

INDEX

Alexander, Gregory, 149n25
Alexy, Robert, 209n10
Ashe, Marie, 147n5
Bakkan, Joel, 147n4
Balkin, Jack, 127, 130, 147n4,
  147n5, 148n7, 149n15,
  152n38, 208n7
Barnett, Randy, 177
Beatty, David, 209n10
Belleau, Marie-Claire, 171n12,
  209n13
Berman, Nathaniel, 147n5
Bix, Brian, 165-70, 170n1,
  171n6, 173n30, 173n37
Blackstone, William, 135
Bourdieu, Pierre, 202, 210n28
Boyle, James, 147n4, 148n5, 167,
  173n32
Burke, Edmund, 198
Butler, Judith, 140
Cardozo, Benjamin, 180, 208n3
Caruso, Daniela, 208n1, 210n20
Casebeer, Kenneth, 149n25
Chafee, Zachariah,130, 149n21
Cohen, Felix, 1, 85n1
Crenshaw, Kimberle, 148n5
Dalton, Clare, 148n5
Demogue, René, 137
Derrida, Jacques, 136, 137,
  143-44
Duxbury, Neil, 148n8
Dworkin, Ronald, 168, 173n34,
  177
Feuerbach, Ludwig, 6
Feyerabend, Paul, 210n26
Fineman, Jay, 150n25
Fisher, William, 150n25

Flores, Imer, 170n1
Forbath, William, 149n25
Foucault, Michel, 202, 210n30,
  210n31
Freeman, Alan, 150n25
Freud, Anna, 163, 172n25
Freud, Sigmund, 132, 163,
  172n24
Fried, Charles, 177
Frug, Gerald,147n4, 150n25
Frug, Mary Joe, 148n5
Gabel, Peter, 150n25
Gény, Francois, 156, 171n10
Gianformaggio, Letizia, 171n5
Gordon, Robert, 147n4, 150n25,
  210n22
Habermas, Jurgen, 162, 172n21,
  183, 187, 209n11
Hager, Mark, 150n25
Hand, Learned, 130
Hart, Henry, 135, 136
Hart, Herbert, 5, 154-158,
  164, 165, 169, 171n2, 171n3,
  171n6, 171n7, 171n9, 172n13,
  173n38
Hartog, Hendrik, 149n25
Heidt, Robert, 147n4
Heller, Thomas, 148n5
Hesselink, Martijn, 9, 208n1
Hohfeld, Wesley, 100, 102, 130,
  149n16
Holmes, Oliver Wendell, 49,
  130, 149n18, 149n19
Horwitz, Morton, 149n25
Hurvitz, Hagai, 150n25
Husserl, Edmund, 1, 158, 161,
  172n16, 172n19

Jacobson, Arthur, 150n25
Jaff, Jennifer, 147n4
Jhering, Rudolf von, 137
Kainen, James, 150n25
Kant, Immanuel, 170, 186, 189
Katz, Al, 150n25
Kelman, Ellen, 150n25
Kelman, Mark, 42,147n4,
    151n26, 166, 173n30
Kelsen, Hans, 5, 154-158, 164,
    165, 171n2, 171n4, 171n7,
    171n8, 172n14, 172n26
Kennedy, David, 147n4, 148n5,
    150n25
Kerchove, Marthe van de,
    209n10
Kessler, Friedrich, 139
Kierkegaard, Soren, 189
Klare, Karl, 150n25, 208n5
Kohler, Wolfgang, 85n1, 158,
    172n18
Kramer, Matthew, 147n5
Krauss, Eugene, 150n25
Levi, Edward H., 1, 85n1
Levi-Strauss, Claude, 127-134,
    148n10, 149n14, 152n31, 198
Lewin, Kurt, 85n1
Llewellyn, Karl, 1, 2, 85n1, 127,
    148n9
Lopez, Diego Eduardo, 210n35
Lupoi, Maurizio, 210n32
Macaulay, Stewart, 177
MacCormick, Neil, 164, 165,
    172n27
Macneil, Ian, 177
Mannheim, Karl, 162, 172n22
Marcuse, Herbert, 210n24
Marella, Maria-Rosaria, 208n1
Markesinis, Basil, 210n23
Marx, Karl, 6, 85n1, 132, 146,

158, 169, 172n17
May, James, 150n25
Mensch, Elizabeth, 151n25
Michelman, Frank, 149n17
Milun, David, 148n5
Minda, Gary, 151n25
Minow, Martha, 148n5
Mitchell, W., 148n5
Mussolini, Benito, 178
Nerkin, Ira, 151n25
Nicola, Fernanda, 209n18
Nietzsche, Friedrich, 189, 199,
    210n29
Nockleby, John, 151n25
Olsen, Frances, 148n5, 151n25,
    208n6
Ost, Francois, 209n10
Paul, Jeremy, 147n4
Paulson, Stanley, 171n5
Peller, Gary, 148n5, 151n25
Perelman, Chaim,135, 137
Peritz, Rudolph, 149n22,
    151n25
Piaget, Jean, 85n1, 130-32, 136,
    149n23, 149n24, 152n27,
    152n28
Posner, Richard, 177
Raz, Joseph, 184-85, 197-98,
    208n9
Rodríguez, César, 9
Rogers, Kipp, 149n22, 151n25
Sacco, Rodolfo, 202, 210n27
Sacks, Albert, 135, 136
Sartre, Jean-Paul, 1, 85n1, 163,
    172n23
Saussure, Ferdinand de, 1, 119,
    129-30, 136, 147n1, 149n13,
    197
Savigny, Friedrich von, 156,
    171n11, 181, 198, 199

Schlag, Pierre, 147n4, 148n5
Schmitt, Karl, 189
Siegel, Stephen, 151n25
Simon, William, 151n25
Singer, Joseph, 149n17, 151n25
Solum, Lawrence, 166, 173n30
Stalin, Joseph, 204
Steinbeck, John, 14
Steinfeld, Robert, 149n25,
    151n25
Stone, Katherine, 151n25
Tarullo, Daniel, 151n25
Teubner, Gunther, 211n36
Torres, Gerald, 148n5
Tushnet, Mark, 149n25
Unger, Roberto, 16, 168,
    173n31
Vandevelde, Kenneth, 151n25
Walras, Leon, 119
Weber, Max, 8, 161, 189,
    208n10
Wieacker, Franz, 178, 181,
    208n2
Wittgenstein, Ludwig, 81, 137,
    142-45

Made in the USA
Lexington, KY
14 February 2011